TWAYNE'S WORLD AUTHORS SERIES

A Survey of the World's Literature

Sylvia E. Bowman, Indiana University

GENERAL EDITOR

SPAIN

Gerald Wade, Vanderbilt University

EDITOR

Manuel Tamayo y Baus

(TWAS 263)

TWAYNE'S WORLD AUTHORS SERIES (TWAS)

The purpose of TWAS is to survey the major writers —novelists, dramatists, historians, poets, philosophers, and critics—of the nations of the world. Among the national literatures covered are those of Australia, Canada, China, Eastern Europe, France, Germany, Greece, India, Italy, Japan, Latin America, the Netherlands, New Zealand, Poland, Russia, Scandinavia, Spain, and the African nations, as well as Hebrew, Yiddish, and Latin Classical literatures. This survey is complemented by Twayne's United States Authors Series and English Authors Series.

The intent of each volume in these series is to present a critical-analytical study of the works of the writer; to include biographical and historical material that may be necessary for understanding, appreciation, and critical appraisal of the writer; and to present all material in clear, concise English—but not to vitiate the scholarly content of the work by doing so.

Manuel Tamayo y Baus

By GERARD FLYNN
University of Wisconsin-Milwaukee

Twayne Publishers, Inc.   ::   New York

8/1973
Genl Cont

FOR EMMA
WITH LOVE

Note to the Reader

Almost all the quotations of Tamayo's plays are taken from the *Obras completas,* Ediciones Fax (Madrid, 1947). I have used the abbreviation *OC* to refer to this text. For example:

OC, 972 means *Obras completas,* page 972.

OC, 972, 12 means *Obras completas,* page 972, line 12.

Preface

The purpose of this book is to introduce the reader to the Spanish playwright, Manuel Tamayo y Baus (1829-1898). The first chapter emphasizes his biography, the following chapters his theater, the last chapter his aesthetics. For insights into his life, I have relied on many documents recently edited and published by Dr. Ramón Esquer Torres, the foremost *tamayista*. In most of the chapters I have referred to Tamayo's Carlism and religious beliefs because he constantly shows a preference for the Church and the *ancien régime*. Tamayo was also the popularizer of a stern, fundamentalist theology.

The past criticism of Tamayo, which has not been plentiful, has usually been confined to a statement of facts about his life and a series of descriptions of his plays. A good part of the criticism resembles the 1898 necrology of Tamayo's friend, Alejandro Pidal y Mon; the notable exceptions to this statement are described in the Selected Bibliography.

This book includes several long quotations from Tamayo, and also two appendices consisting of letters he wrote to the Carlist electorate and Don Carlos de Borbón, the pretender to the throne. As far as I know, they are unobtainable elsewhere in English translation. I hope they will give the reader a fair idea of Tamayo's literature and of his allegiance to the *ancien régime*. Unless otherwise indicated, all translations are my own.

As Chapter 6 indicates, a list of Tamayo's plays will run from thirty-five to fifty titles, depending on how many titles the compiler includes of plays adapted from the French. I myself have discussed twenty-three titles in this book, eighteen from the *Obras completas (Complete Works)* of the 1947 Fax edition, and five from the Oberlin College *Spanish Drama Collection*. I have explained my reason for this choice in Chapter 6. If the reader wishes, he can also consult the four-volume *Obras (Works)* of 1898-1900, which are listed in the Selected Bibliography.

The seventh chapter is a study of the aesthetics Tamayo set forth in his Royal Academy speech of June 12, 1859. As I have observed in this chapter, Tamayo wrote his best plays when he followed his own aesthetics. Unfortunately, he did not always follow them.

The Selected Bibliography has comments on many critics of Tamayo, which the reader can supplement with other comments in the body of the book and in the *Notes and References*. The translations in the appendices and all the translations from Tamayo's letters and Academy speech are my own.

I wish to thank my colleagues at the University of Wisconsin-Milwaukee, Professor Oliver Myers and Professor Alfred Rodríguez, for their help and encouragement, particularly in questions of translation and Tamayo's aesthetics.' I should also like to thank Professor John Kronik of Cornell University for his generous help and for reading the chapter on aesthetics. And I am grateful to Professor Gerald Wade of Vanderbilt University for his loyal criticism.

Above all, I want to mention my debt to my wife, who has read my manuscript more than four times.

GERARD FLYNN

University of Wisconsin-Milwaukee

Contents

Chronology

1829   September 15: Manuel Tamayo y Baus was born in Madrid of parents who were actors.

1847   The opening of his first play, *Juana de Arco (Joan of Arc)*, which was based on Schiller's *The Maid of Orleans*.

1849   Married María Emilia Máiquez, his "Amalia."

1852   *Ángela*, a play based on Schiller's *Love and Intrigue*.

1853   *Virginia*, a tragedy in five acts. His own favorite play.

1854   *La ricahembra (Doña Juana the Magnate)*, a play based on the *romances* (Spanish ballads).

1855   *La locura de amor (The Madness of Love)*. One of his most famous plays, about the mad queen of Castile, Doña Juana la loca.

1856   *La bola de nieve (The Snowball)*. A play about jealousy. The last play he wrote in verse.

1858   Elected to the Royal Academy of Language.

1859   Read his discourse on aesthetics, "Truth Considered as the Source of Beauty in Dramatic Literature," on his formal reception into the Royal Academy. *Lo positivo (The Right Track)*. A play denouncing nineteenth-century positivism. The beginning of Tamayo's *alta comedia*.

1863   *Lances de honor (Duels of Honor)*. A thesis drama against dueling.

1867   *Un drama nuevo (A New Drama)*. His masterpiece.

1870   *Los hombres de bien (The Upright Men)*. His last play.

1870-   Twenty-eight years of silence in the theater.
1898

1871   Ran unsuccessfully for public office on the Carlist ticket.

1874   Elected Executive Secretary of the Royal Academy of Language. An indefatigable worker at his official tasks.

1884   Became Director of the National Library. Was extremely active in this office.

1898   Died in the arms of his wife, "Amalia."

CHAPTER 1

The Nineteenth-Century Playwright

I Introduction

THE spiritual division in Spain during the last two centuries, the enmity between traditionalists and liberals,
might well be called the Great Spanish Dichotomy. The
traditionalists, who believe in "God, King and Country," have
staunchly supported the Church, whereas the liberals, who
represent modern, democratic ideals, have generally opposed the
Church. The lines of this dichotomy are not always rigid within
the lives of men; for example, the liberal crusader Benito Pérez
Galdós[1] (1843-1920) was a close friend of the conservative
Carlist, José María Pereda (1833-1906), and the resolute Catholic, Marcelino Menéndez Pelayo (1856-1912), fought tooth and
nail to have Galdós admitted into the Royal Academy; but by
and large the lines in public life are rigid indeed. To understand
modern Spain, one must study this dichotomy, which more than
any other factor of Spanish life gave rise to the civil wars of
1833-1839, 1872-1876, and 1936-1939.

The famous playwright Manuel Tamayo y Baus (1829-1898)
typifies the traditionalist half of the Spanish Dichotomy.
He believed in the Church and its authority and in the close
bonds of the family; he believed in the Crown and its authority
and in the Carlist pretender to the throne, Carlos de Borbón;
and he believed in his *patria*, his country, which rested securely
on the pillars of Crown and Church. Even in aesthetics his credo
was "man, and above man, God," an affirmation that frequently
appears in the thesis dramas he wrote. At times his traditionalism is extremely didactic, and although it makes his thesis dramas
interesting historical documents, it now detracts from them as
literature.

Tamayo was born, lived, and died within the sacraments of

13

his Church. When he was forty-three years old, he ran for office
on the Carlist ticket and published an open letter[2] that is a
model of monarchical sentiment. During the last twenty-eight
years of his life he retired from the theater and served his
country as permanent secretary of the Royal Academy of Language and as Director of the National Library. His death in
1898 symbolizes the demise of Old Spain, much as does the
loss of the colonies to the United States or the appearance of the
new *casticismo* (Spanish essence) of Don Miguel de Unamuno.

II *Tamayo's Family*

Manuel Tamayo y Baus was born in Madrid on September
15, 1829. According to his baptismal certificate, he was given the
sacrament the very next day in the Church of San Sebastián,
in the arms of his maternal aunt and godmother, Teresa Baus.
San Sebastián symbolized the theatrical as well as the religious
aspirations of the baby's parents, for it had been a favorite
parish of the great actors and playwrights of the Golden Age
in Spain. Lope de Vega was buried there.[3]

Tamayo was born into a family of actors. His father, Don
José Tamayo, was a leading man and director in the theaters
outside of Madrid, especially in Granada, Sevilla, Cádiz, and
Málaga, all of them major cities of Andalucía, Spain's southern-
most province. As a result of this long residence in the south of
Spain, the boy Manuel always felt a strong attachment to the
region. His friends Manuel Cañete and Luis and Aureliano Fernández-Guerra were from that area; his wife, "Amalia," daughter
of the play producer José Máiquez, also came from there, and
years later in the Royal Academy of Language Tamayo and
his friends formed "The Granada Group."

Tamayo's mother, Joaquina Baus, was a leading lady who,
more than anyone else, set her son's sights on a career as a playwright. She taught him to read and recite passages from the
classics of the theater, and to gesture with his hands and body.
By her own example, she taught him to love all the theatrical
arts. His most satisfying moment in the theater took place on
the night of October 21, 1847, when his mother played the
part of Joan in his first play, *Juana de Arco* (*Joan of Arc*).[4] Her

devoted son, barely nineteen years old at the time, was never to forget this triumph. Tamayo's father played the part of Joan of Arc's father, Thibaut.

Tamayo had three younger brothers and sisters, Andrés, Victorino, and Josefa. Andrés enjoyed some small success as a playwright, although his name would be forgotten now were it not for his association with his older brother. Victorino became a well-known actor in his own right and played a leading role in most of Tamayo's plays, the most famous of which was Yorick in *Un drama nuevo* (*A New Drama*).[5] Tamayo's sister, Josefa, who did not figure in the annals of the theater, maintained a close family tie with him until her death in 1894. Tamayo himself had an extremely strong sense of family.

III *His Education*

Tamayo's childhood in a family of actors that often moved about had a profound effect on his schooling. There is no discussion of this phase of his life in any of the letters, eulogies, necrologies, or histories of the nineteenth century, but the person who studies Tamayo closely can draw several conclusions from later events in his life.

In the first place, Tamayo never learned to read German, although he knew Schiller's plays and used them as models for his *Joan of Arc* and *Ángela*. In an undated letter, written to Menéndez Pelayo some time after 1881[6] (it was in that year that this famous scholar became a member of the Academy of Language), Tamayo penned the following words:

Young pup of my heart: Since you know everything, you must know German; and knowing it, why not take the trouble of translating into Spanish the poetry Fastenrath has sent to the Academy, which I enclose? Isn't that the least the Corporation can do for that mameluke?

You must know I am not asking you to translate it into verse, but into plain, simple prose and a good style.

But by the nails of Christ, don't lose it. Receive a strong embrace from your least worthy companion, in fair weather and foul.[7]

Tamayo read Schiller, probably in the prose translations of M. X. Marmier (*Théâtre de Schiller* [Paris, 1841]). He also read

Hegel's *Poetics* in French, which he used in preparing his Academy entrance speech of 1858.[8]

Tamayo, moreover, knew very little Latin. In another undated letter to Menéndez Pelayo, written after 1881, he wrote:

Most adorable Marcelino: Why do you know so much and why are you an Academician of the Language if not to write in Horace's language the answer that must be sent to this gentleman who has lowered the boom on us with the enclosed letter in Latin?

If I tried to Latin it, it would really be a dark hour for me, and I'd probably die in the attempt.

So you had better do it and take care!

And don't go and lose the evidence!

And leave the neighbors' wives in peace, and pardon and command your friend, *usque ad aras.*

Menéndez Pelayo, who wrote odes to Horace in Latin when he was seventeen years old, had such an unusual command of that language that almost any member of the Academy would have deferred to him on it. Nevertheless, this letter of Tamayo shows that he himself probably had little training in Latin, a year or two perhaps from a tutor, or by irregular schooling.[9] The historical records are silent on the subject.

There is no reason to suppose that Tamayo read either English or Italian fluently, although he was familiar with Shakespeare's plays and Alfieri's; there is no record of his translating their works. On the other hand, he must have been at home in French, for he often translated and made adaptations of French plays and novels. One source mentions a total of fourteen plays arranged from the French.[10]

On April 2, 1844, when he was fourteen years old, Tamayo sent a letter to Manuel Cañete that throws some light on his schooling:

... if a very long experience of uninterrupted studies has not made it sufficiently clear to him that the University is a trifle and he who goes there a fool, I, who do not consider myself a fool since I have not placed a foot in it, not one single time, in my career thus far; I say, I can tell that gentleman something he seems not to know even after such long experience, namely, that the creative gift does not need crutches, or what amounts to the same thing or is at least similar, that we have for a disciple the congressman Mr. Pom. Horrors! Terror and fury! Common sense has been on vacation ever since they opened the classrooms, and with good reason . . .[11]

This passage suggests that Tamayo's education was largely autodidactic. Even allowing for the exuberance of a teen-age boy, one must admit he has a bias against the rigors and plodding ways of a schoolroom. He was accustomed to more spontaneous, intuitive flights of the imagination.

In summary, the young Tamayo's schooling seems to have consisted largely of the example and direction of his parents, his experiences within the theater, the voracious reading in translation of the plays of many countries, a specialization in the Spanish theater, the French language, and some Latin, perhaps two years of it. He must have had tutoring, if only that of his parents, and it is problematical whether or not he went to school. When he was fourteen years old, he looked forward to more and more theatrical experience rather than university training, and he was a tireless worker. On reaching manhood, he possessed a sound literary education.

IV *His Marriage and Career*

On September 14, 1849, the eve of his twentieth birthday, Tamayo married María Emilia Máiquez (his Amalia), daughter of a famous impresario. She became his companion of fifty years and he always paid her the highest devotion. Her image and the image he retained of his mother are the models of many female characters in his plays.

About this time, Antonio Gil y Zárate, a famous playwright and a relative of Tamayo by marriage, gave him a small position in the civil service. Tamayo always had some sort of public employment from this time until his death, except for short periods after 1854 and 1868 when liberal politicians availed themselves of the Spanish spoils system to turn him and other conservatives into *cesantes*. The *cesante*, the unemployed public servant, is a familiar figure in nineteenth-century Spain.[12] Tamayo was not the completely apolitical figure that some critics have made him out to be.

During his first creative decade, 1847-1856, Tamayo wrote

about ten outstanding dramas. He based the first two of these
on Schiller's *The Maiden of Orleans* and *Love and Intrigue*.
Then he made an attempt at tragedy in his own favorite play,
Virginia; after that he turned to history, in *La ricahembra*
(*Doña Juana the Magnate*) and *La locura de amor* (*The Madness of Love*); and finally he turned to plays showing his concern for moral issues. This concern was to gain ascendancy in
his second creative decade, 1862-1870, when he wrote several of
the most famous thesis[13] plays of the nineteenth century. And it
was in 1867 that he wrote his renowned *Un drama nuevo* (*A
New Drama*).

Throughout both creative decades, Tamayo continued translating plays and making adaptations from the French, since this
was where the money lay, and neither he nor the members of his
company could ignore its appeal. There was no Bohemianism
in Tamayo or his associates, who did not try to create art and
lead the free life at the same time. He was by all accounts a successful businessman.

On March 18, 1858, Tamayo experienced the most important
event of his public life. He was voted "a member of number,"
that is, a member with a chair, in the Spanish Royal Academy
of Language. He seems to have cherished this honor, and the
Academy became for him rather like a second bride. As an
academician, he could sit beside his lifelong friends, Manuel
Cañete and Luis and Aureliano Fernández-Guerra, and mingle
with such luminaries as the playwrights Manuel Bretón de los
Herreros (1796-1873) and Adelardo López de Ayala (1828-
1879), the novelists Don Juan Valera (1824-1905), Pedro Antonio
de Alarcón (1833-1891), and José María Pereda (1833-1906),
the critic Marcelino Menéndez Pelayo (1856-1912), the poets
Gaspar Núñez de Arce (1834-1903) and José Zorrilla (1817-
1893), and the author, politician and orator, Emilio Castelar
(1832-1899). Tamayo established far and away the best attendance record in the Academy's history,[14] and in 1874 he became
its Executive Secretary. He conscientiously discharged the many
duties of this post, for example, the revision of the Academy's
Dictionary, until his death in 1898.[15] He was also Director of
the National Library after 1884.

There remain to be discussed in this biographical sketch Tamayo's Carlism, the question of his use of pseudonyms from 1862 to 1870, his long silence from 1870 to 1898, and the final destruction of his papers.

V *Tamayo's Carlism*

Carlism, another label for traditionalism, is the term often applied to the counterrevolutionary movement in Spain in the nineteenth century. It attracted all those who chose to consider themselves as disciples of "God, King and Country," who opposed the Press and also any major change toward what we should now call "Progress," who resented the disruption of national Catholic unity; in a word, those who favored the *ancien régime*. It also attracted many Catalonians, Navarrese, and Basques who hoped to maintain their local privileges, their states' rights so to speak, in opposition to the central government of Madrid. The Carlist revolt came to a head in the civil wars of 1833-1839 and 1872-1876.

In 1868, Tamayo was serving as Director of the Library of San Isidro. After the September Revolution of that year, he was discharged from his post, a *cesante por reforma* according to the euphemism of the day, although he himself did not consider it political in nature. An extremely diligent worker, this action hurt him to the quick, so much so that he began to show more interest in the Carlist party, which represented his political and religious sentiments. He also had many friends in that quarter, particularly Cándido Nocedal, his colleague in the Academy and leader of the Carlist party's nonbellicose wing.

In 1871, Tamayo, then forty-one years old, decided to run for office on the Carlist platform. He was prompted to do so by the September Revolution of 1868, by the vacancy of the throne, and finally by the efforts of Generals Prim and Serrano to choose as king a foreigner, to be known as Amadeus I (this new king's reign was fated to last only from 1870 to 1873). In an open letter addressed to his electorate, Tamayo wrote:

Does the liberal monarchy please you? Take a good look at it. The heresy of Luther triumphant over the Catholic Church; religious unity taken away from all Spaniards for the benefit of a few Protestants or atheists, who being atheists or Protestants, are not Spaniards

though they were born in Spain; the liberty of evil applauded and
recognized and for that very reason the liberty of good denied and
struck down, because good men and bad men cannot be free at
one and the same time; power, exercised in the name of reason,
rebelling against faith, the insufferable and barbarous tyranny of
man over man. The means of repression? These two exclusively:
insidious corruption and brutal force. . . . At all times the suffering
of horrendous evils, and when not suffering them, the rightful fearing
of still greater ones . . .

Do you prefer the Catholic Monarchy? The Monarchy that, embracing the Church of Jesus Christ, governs in the name of eternal
principles; that is not free to contaminate and much less to suppress;
imposing on men not the yoke of another man but the most sweet
and holy yoke of the truth and the justice that come from God, by
which rule is legitimate and obedience easy, and both rule and
obedience are jointly ennobled and exalted? . . . In that case vote
for me. I say to you: "I am a Catholic and therefore a Carlist."[16]

The reader will notice the plethora of adjectives in this political pamphlet (see Appendix 1, where it appears in its entirety).
Soberness of epithet is lacking: "*insidious* corruption," "*brutal*
force," "*horrendous* evils," "*insufferable* debt," "*enormous* expenses, "*enormous* machine," "*scandalous* success," "*incredible*
abuses," "*perpetual* and *fratricidal* war," "*lamentable* state." All
these adjectives might be called words-in-reverse,[17] for they do
not reflect external reality so much as the exaggerated quality of
the emotions within Tamayo's breast. There is no doubt that the
liberal governments of Spain were culpable of abuses, but Tamayo sees in these governments a sort of evil incarnate, an absolute. If such an evil were possible, then a person of course must
spare no adjectives to describe it, for no one adjective or noun
would suffice; just as God is called omnipotent, omniscient, omni-
present and so forth, so the Liberal Machine must be called all-
insidious, all-brutal, all-horrendous. Tamayo's Manichaean[18]
vision of politics was undoubtedly sincere, for nowhere in his
life's story is there evidence of deviousness on his part. A more
malign Carlist might use a pamphlet such as this to harangue
the people, but not Tamayo. It follows his political vision, which
sees the adversary poisoning everything, and his own party imposing a biblical yoke, "most sweet and holy."[19]

In addition to the adjectives, there are other statements of this political letter that catch the reader's eye. The reference to the great warrior and ruler, St. Fernando III, who once held the Spanish throne, provides another insight into Tamayo's thoughts. His country, his fatherland, his family, his town ("the families and the towns") are inseparable from his religious credo, and their indissoluble union was symbolized by the monarch-saint, Don Fernando. No foreigner such as Amadeus can rule this Spain; it is not only undesirable that he do so, it is impossible. An atheist certainly cannot rule Spain, he least of all, and here perhaps Tamayo is thinking of a man like Francisco Pi y Margall (1824-1901).[20] Protestants are perhaps less reprehensible than atheists, but again they are foreigners who are not and cannot be the sons of St. Fernando. The heterodox novelist, Galdós, may people his thesis novels with fanatical Catholics and benign agnostics, but Galdós himself, by his very heterodoxy, is not a Spaniard and consequently he is incapable of understanding Spain.

The reader who wishes to understand the politico-religious credo of Tamayo would do well to read two novels. First, the *Don Juan* of Azorín (José Martínez Ruiz, 1873-1967), in which the lovable, blind holy bishop tells how he saw the Enemy once in France many years ago, the Enemy, Ernest Renan.[21] He should also read Ramón del Valle-Inclán's (1866-1936) *Los cruzados de la causa* (*Crusaders for the Cause*), the opening novel of the author's *Carlist War* trilogy, in which many devout, xenophobic people make sacrifices for the crusade of Don Carlos de Borbón. Tamayo resembles both the bishop and these people. He was a sincere, devout man who had a certain limitation of vision.

VI   *The Pseudonyms, The Long Silence, The Destruction of Tamayo's Papers*

For three years after his entrance into the Royal Academy in 1859, Tamayo was much less active as a playwright than he had been in the previous decade, but beginning with *Lo positivo* (*The Right Track*) in 1862, until *Los hombres de bien* (*The Upright Men*) in 1870, he wrote a series of seven plays and also some arrangements and translations. These works constitute almost half of his theater.

It is remarkable that in this second creative decade, the 1860's, Tamayo signed his plays with pseudonyms—Joaquín Estébanez, José María García, Don Fulano de Tal, Juan del Peral—rather than his own famous name. Students and admirers of Tamayo have often asked themselves *why?*[22]

Tamayo's favorite pseudonym, the one he affixed to his best plays, including *Un drama nuevo* (*A New Drama*), was Joaquín Estébanez. His reason for choosing this name was made clear during his lifetime by Isidoro Fernández Flórez. Writing on September 20, 1884, this critic said:

. . . the public, completely won over by the work (*Lo positivo*) called for the author many times. Don Joaquín Estébanez? Who is that gentleman, everyone was asking? And the connoisseurs of literature replied: Who else? Tamayo! Then someone realized that the famous actress Baus was called Joaquina and that Estébanez was her maiden name.[23]

Thus, in signing his plays "Joaquín Estébanez," Tamayo was honoring the memory of his mother, Joaquina Baus, née Estébanez, whom he idolized.

The overall question, however, remains: why did Tamayo turn to the use of pseudonyms whenever he staged a new play? Some observers have argued an inbred modesty on his part. Others have suggested that after he became a member of the Academy, the institution he revered, he did not want to identify his name with a work of doubtful outcome lest the critics in judging him also judge the Academy; some of his thesis plays had been jeered at, and he was unwilling to have the Academy risk such abuse. Before advancing a third possible answer, which by no means precludes the two just mentioned, it would be well to discuss Tamayo's silence and the final destruction of his papers.

By December of 1870, when he was forty-one years old, Tamayo had become the most famous playwright in Spain. Just three years before, he had staged his most successful play, *A New Drama*; he had also staged plays in 1868 and 1870. Nevertheless, that December he laid down his pen, never to pick it up again in the last twenty-eight years of his life. He revised his favorite drama, *Virginia,* apparently for his own satisfaction, but he wrote nothing further for the theater.

This unusual silence on Tamayo's part is complicated by his last will, which was a verbal rather than a written testament.[24] He took several file cases and filled them with manuscripts, rough sketches, memoranda concerning his speeches, notes about his academic chores and principal plays, and a few other papers. These files he left to his widow, who in turn donated them to the library of the Royal Academy. But he had privately asked a son of his brother, Victorino, to destroy all his other papers. The dearth of documents concerning Tamayo today shows how efficiently his nephew carried out his will.

Why did Tamayo use pseudonyms, maintain a long silence, and order his papers destroyed? It is this destruction, of course, that makes a definitive answer impossible. He may have been an exceptionally modest man, he may have wanted to protect his beloved Academy from abuse, he may have found the tasks of Executive Secretary and Library Director more to his liking in his middle years, he may have had many other reasons for seeking such anonymity. But none of these "may haves" carries the stamp of certitude. Given Tamayo's religious convictions, one might simply argue that he removed himself from the scene for ascetic reasons. Self-denial awakens a man to the ultimate knowledge that this world is a dream, a vestibule to our eternal dwelling place. In the words of Jorge Manrique (1440-1479):

> This world is but the rugged road
> Which leads us to the bright abode
> Of peace above;
> . . . .
> There all are equal. Side by side
> The poor man and the son of pride
> Lie calm and still.[25]

CHAPTER 2

Tamayo Moralizes

I Introduction

THE poor man and the son of pride were the favorite characters of Don Manuel Tamayo y Baus, who wrote several moral plays about them.[1] Apparently these plays became for him a mode of expressing his deepest political and religious convictions, for they correspond to the meaning and form of the Carlist letters.[2] They also correspond to the stern, didactic manner Tamayo displayed later in life.[3] In this sense, the moral plays are Tamayo's most representative theater. They deserve to have first mention in a study of the present kind.

II The Moral Plays

Lo positivo (*The Right Track*), 1862
Lances de honor (*Duels of Honor*), 1863
Del dicho al hecho (*Actions Speak Louder*), 1863
No hay mal que por bien no venga
                 (*Every Evil Hath Its Good*), 1868
Los hombres de bien (*The Upright Men*), 1870

In the opening speech of *The Right Track*,[4] Rafael states the conflict. Cecilia is pretty:

But, as always, so fond of display and so taken with money. . . . She follows the maxims of her father, a zealous adorer of the golden ox. Cursed money, which so prostitutes and poisons noble hearts. (*OC*, 721, 9)

The message is blunt. Everything is stated in black and white. Noble hearts, or spirits, soar, whereas money, or matter, drags the spirit down into the mud. This is similar to the Manichaean[6]

24

vision of Tamayo in his letter condemning the Liberals and praising the Carlists.

Two scenes later, Cecilia's uncle, the marquis, puts the meaning of Rafael's blunt statement into other words:

You must remember that in the century we live in everyone has come to believe that happiness is something you buy with money. . . . We, Rafael, had a noble model to imitate in the duke, your father and my older brother. He transmitted to us the ideas and sentiments of other ages, which today are called barbarous . . .[6] (*OC*, 724, 15)

Here is the key to the real Tamayo. He is the eternal *laudator temporis acti;* he is Virgil or Horace lamenting the decline of Rome; he is Don Quijote contemplating the acorns and telling the goatherds that we live in a detestable age of iron where everything is *thine* and *mine,* but there was a day when these words did not exist and young damsels walked across meadow and sward unmolested. This was the golden age, when everyone lived the doctrine of the Sermon on the Mount, like "the duke your father and my older brother." This nostalgic lament of Tamayo is an outstanding feature of nineteenth-century literature. The *costumbristas*[7] tell us, with Tamayo, that the good things are succumbing; a famous novelist like Pereda wrote several regional novels on the same theme; and as late as 1911, Armando Palacio Valdés tells his readers that *La aldea perdida* (*The Lost Village*), the village of his youth, is a vanished Arcadia, that the mountain boys were good, true, clean, hearty, rustic lads whereas the men of modern factories and mines are a bunch of sotted Plutos. Things were better in the old days![8]

In crying out the glories of the past through his moral plays Tamayo was proving himself a good traditionalist, and most literate Spaniards agreed with him.[9] This cry was to be challenged by men of great stature, the most eminent of whom was Galdós (1843-1920). Unfortunately for Spain, the issue was still unsettled as late as 1936, the year in which the great Civil War began.

In one line of the play, Rafael, an army officer on leave of absence, addresses the following words to a materialistic relative:

You forget, uncle, that I went to fight for my religion, my country, and my queen.

These words correspond to the traditionalist motto of "God, King and Country."

At one point, Cecilia makes a pun. She is describing a wealthy man she may marry, a most unattractive character:

However, he carries on like a good lad, because, yes, he has very good coloring, too good. Also he is a little fat . . . rather fat . . . really fat. . . . But his very obesity gives him a certain character, that of a man of great weight. (*OC*, 733, 41)

The Spanish word for weight is *peso*, which is also a unit of money. This kind of word play and jocularity is rare in Tamayo, except in his early one-act plays (which will receive consideration later in the present study). After Cecilia's *peso* speech, Rafael immediately gets back to Tamayo's condemnation of "that infamous thirst for gold" and his praise of "the holy joy of the family."

Toward the end of the play (Act III, Scene vii), Tamayo resorts to an image of the business world in speaking of the deity. Rafael has inherited a fortune, and now, what will he do with it? His good uncle, the marquis, advises him:

MARQUIS. Use your money in much better investments than mines and railroads, and put it in the hands of a banker who pays incalculable interest.
RAFAEL. I don't understand.
MARQUIS. That banker, who is called God, never makes all the payments good until the next life, but at times he concedes in this life some recompense in advance. (*OC*, 779, 24)

Likening God to a banker and his creature to an investor is a crass positivistic metaphor that seems out of place in a play attacking social positivism. It shows that, in the long run, even Tamayo the traditionalist is a child of his time, the nineteenth century. He may denounce materialism, but he cannot help using its lexicon.[10]

The Right Track ends well. Cecilia is on the verge of marrying a ruthless millionaire when love wins out and she accepts the impecunious Rafael. But it happens that Rafael is to inherit a huge fortune, left him by a dying friend, and everyone speaks of using it to help the poor.

Tamayo's moral plays usually end with the *deus ex machina,* a sudden spiritual conversion or an unforeseen inheritance. They were written by the Tamayo of the Happy Ending.

III Lances de honor (Duels of Honor)

The same Madrid bourgeoisie that flocked to see Tamayo's other moral plays had mixed feelings about *Duels of Honor.* A good part of the audience was outraged, not entertained. The French critic, Boris de Tannenberg, has made the following observation:

Political and antireligious passion alone kept the public in 1863 from applauding in Spain one of the most beautiful dramas [*Duels of Honor*] of this author. . . . For me it is the strongest thesis play that Spain has produced in this whole century. That is what this powerful drama is, admirable for the severe art of its composition, even at a first glance. There is nothing in it outside the main point. Not even one love story to distract or mislead the audience's interest. Not one useless character.[11]

Duels of Honor, which has a more specific thesis than the other moral plays, is not concerned with entertaining the audience. It has a fixed point of view. It has "nothing in it outside the main point." There is something obsessive about it, for the author has to single out one question in particular, dueling, and attack it. Perhaps he himself was challenged to a duel and on declining was called a coward; perhaps he was thinking of the famous duel of Pedro Antonio de Alarcón (1833-1891);[12] perhaps he saw good men in the Spanish Parliament obliged to duel for a political conviction; perhaps he simply felt it was his God-given mission to erase this evil from the face of the earth— in any case, he, Tamayo, was determined personally to wipe out dueling.[13] His drama must grip the audience and as long as it does that, less serious entertainment is of little account.

Fortunately for students of Tamayo today, the playwright José Echegaray attended the opening night of *Duels of Honor.* In his memoirs he describes what he saw.[14]

Echegaray says he has seen all the opening nights of Tamayo, from the "great triumph" of *Angela* (1852), to the "enormous battle" over *Los hombres de bien* (*The Upright Men*) in 1870.

He says he never knew Tamayo throughout this period, although
he admired him, and later they became friends.

Echegaray continues:

I remember, among other premieres, that of his admirable drama,
Duels of Honor, which is, as I see it, one of his best creations. And
I remember the premiere of this work as if it were just yesterday;
and I recall with lively indignation the irritating injustice of that
audience.

The audience apparently was deeply moved by the play and
might have accepted it except for something that happened in
the last act. Echegaray continues his account:

How explain that a drama, which during three or four acts[15] goes
up and down amid applauses and protests, arrives at the final scene
and is, so to speak, hanging on a hair! How explain that it can be
broken in a moment, and less than a moment, in an instant! That the
balance of dramatic justice be hanging on a needle point, that it can
just as readily go to the right or the left, and that the last sentence
alone is strong enough to make the balance fall into the plate on the
sinister [left] side! But only a biased audience, unjust, irascible,
fanatical in its own way, because there are many types of fanaticism,
is capable of rejecting literary works of extraordinary merit because of
one sentence alone! And *Duels of Honor* has such merit.

Echegaray goes on to explain the plot of the play and its
thesis. He mentions the famous actors, Joaquín Arjona and
Teodora Lamadrid, who played the principal roles. He remembers that "Pepita Hijosa, then a young girl" had a small role
and that one of the actors, "a fellow named Díaz or Díez" was
applauded by the public.[16] He says that right down to the end
"the work went ahead with full sail and we all expected a great
triumph."

But just before the end, something happened. Teodora
Lamadrid, who was playing the mother of a boy killed in a duel,
said something that offended the audience. In the words of
Echegaray:

But lo and behold, they bring on the stage the magistrate's son,
mortally wounded, and in the desperation of those cruel moments
Teodora pronounces one or two sentences revealing the anguish and

sorrow of the Christian mother who sees her son die in a state of mortal sin for having wanted to kill a fellow human being, and who dies without having received absolution.

This sentence and this sentence alone sufficed to unleash the rage of the audience, so that it forgot all its enthusiasm; and a play that had been a continuous triumph wound up being protested.[17]

The reader today is tempted to ask: which part of the audience put up a fuss at the end, the Catholic part or the anti-Catholic, or both?[18] One can readily see both groups taking offense at the words of Teodora Lamadrid.[19]

IV *The Plot*

The story of *Duels of Honor* concerns two families, Don Pedro de Villena and his son Paulino, and Don Fabián García and his wife and son, Candelaria and Miguel. Both fathers are politicians.

In the Parliament, Don Pedro has accused the Government of a fraudulent election and apparently it will fall. But Don Fabián eloquently answers him and clears the Government of the charge. He has embarrassed Don Pedro, who is guilty of calumny, and the latter challenges him to a duel. Don Fabián declines.

Don Pedro leaves no stone unturned in order to force a duel with his enemy. He insults him in public, sends seconds to challenge him, writes him a letter in which he talks of spitting in his face, goes to his house and insults him privately, and finally slaps him in public.

Don Fabían refuses to fight not out of cowardice, but religious conviction. Many people laugh at him, his old friends turn from him, and even his son is embarrassed at his apparent cowardice. Only his wife, Candelaria, approves of his action.

Finally, Don Fabián is so outraged that he weakens and declares he will duel, but before he does he and Don Pedro learn that their sons, Paulino and Miguel, have decided to duel in their stead. The fathers are united now in their attempt to stop the boys from fighting, but they arrive at the duel site too late. Paulino has mortally wounded Miguel, who forgives him and dies in a Christian manner (though unshriven). At the end, Don Pedro is converted and prays to God.

V *A Criticism*

There can be no doubt that the second act of this play is one
of the best passages Tamayo ever wrote. The characterization of
Don Fabián is a memorable moment in the theater. He starts out
with Christian resignation and refuses to duel. He is an example
of humility. He meets affronts but counters them with simple
well-reasoned arguments. The insults, however, begin to take their
toll. A servant speaks insolently to his wife, and later the same
servant behaves boldly in his presence. A servant, a social inferior,
has let him know that he considers him a coward! His old friend,
Don Dámaso, who knows he is not a coward, tells him that he
will esteem him in private but shun him in public, for such is
the way of the world and he must live in the world. His brother-
in-law, Don Diego, has come to Madrid since Don Pedro
has insulted him also, and he will duel with that scoundrel; in
his own gruff way, he too shows Don Fabián his disapproval.
His son Miguel stutters and vacillates in his presence, although
he will not explicitly disapprove what his father has said or
done. Little by little, they all chip away at Don Fabián's resignation, and finally he changes into a man anxious to avenge
himself. The change has been slow and almost imperceptible.
It was wrought by an author who was a great artist in the theater.

In the third and last act, Tamayo reverts to the Tamayo of
the sudden conversion and the Happy Ending. Everyone is
praying for everyone else and mouthing the name of God,
and there is the shocking scene where the brother-in-law slaps
Don Pedro's face. This has the unfortunate effect of recalling the
venom of the second act and the offstage slapping of Don Fabián
by Don Pedro. The reader feels he is being preached at; how
much more must an audience feel this in the theater![20]

VI *The* Raisonneur

In *Duels of Honor* and the other moral plays, Tamayo employs
a character with an ancient lineage, the *raisonneur*. This French
word means the reasoner or arguer, but in the drama it means
the character who moralizes.[21]

The author who uses a *raisonneur* is not content to let the story of a play speak for itself; rather he acts as if he were writing a parable and then creating a figure whose purpose is to explain the parable. The *raisonneur* is often an older person who stands aside from the main action of a drama and at apt times enters it in order to preach his moral to the audience. In the case of an author like Tamayo, he preaches the values of a traditional order: God, King and Country, and the ethics of the Church; he may also protest against innovation, such as the many economic, political, and social inventions of the nineteenth century. A raisonneur need not be a traditionalist, however. Since he is an author's mouthpiece, in the plays of a liberal such as Galdós he will praise the inventions of the nineteenth century and preach a moral code different than that of the *ancien régime*. In brief, an author who uses a *raisonneur* is not content with example alone. He wants the example spelled out with words.

In *Duels of Honor,* the major *raisonneur* is Don Fabián's wife, Doña Candelaria. She is the perfect wife[22] and she knows whereof she speaks. Dueling is wrong because it is a mortal sin:

Fabián, your life does not belong to you; it belongs to your wife and your son; it belongs above all to God. To die of a bullet at the very moment you are committing a horrible crime! . . . To die without the sacraments . . . perhaps without time to direct one lone look at heaven . . . perhaps blaspheming! (*OC*, 832, 38; and *OC*, 834, 36)

Sometimes it is possible for the victim of injustice himself to moralize and so he becomes a *raisonneur*. This makes the moral more effective since it is closer to the action of the play. Thus, in *Duels of Honor,* when he speaks to his tormentor, Don Fabián makes a more effective moralizer than his wife:

Look: I don't want to duel—you already know why—because I am a fool, an idiot who formally believes that he carries within him an immortal soul; who believes in glory and purgatory and even in hell —laugh as much as you please—who, in a word, believes in God, and still is simple enough to say so. Such reasons—of course—couldn't possibly satisfy you. This business of believing in the God of the catechism is all right for people who aren't too intelligent, people who are weak and despicable; because you men, who pride your-selves on your own will and judgment, know how to make gods that suit the kind of human dignity which scornfully and angrily rejects the yoke of sacred duty; the kind of dignity that humbly accepts ridiculous or vile thoughts.[23] (*OC*, 829, 1)

The *raisonneur* also appears in *The Right Track*, where he is the "good uncle," the marquis.[24] In Act I, Scene iii, one of his first speeches, he tells the other characters and the audience that the worship of money is idolatry and that tradition is opposed to the nineteenth century and superior to it:

You must remember that in the century we live in everyone has come to believe that happiness is something you buy with money. Pablo, who has made his great fortune by his constancy and hard work, cannot help adoring the idol he has sacrificed his entire life to, and like a good businessman, he always carries the account book in his head. We, Rafael, had a noble model to imitate in the duke, your father and my older brother. He transmitted to us the ideas and sentiments of other ages which today are called barbarous, and for this reason, without doubt, we are not now the same as your poor uncle or even worse than he, who has been carried away since his youth by the current of vulgar opinion. (*OC*, 724, 15)

This *raisonneur* of Tamayo preaches righteousness, and his righteousness shapes his rhetoric. This rather long speech consists of only three periods, which carry the ideas along in a grand style.

Another example of the *raisonneur* is Damián Ortiz, the moral young man of Tamayo's last play, *The Upright Men*. He is a thoroughly wooden character, although he occasionally has a fair line:

In every age there is a figure in fashion: the poet, the philosopher, the soldier, the friar, the gentleman. . . . And now, the scoundrel is the latest rage. (*OC*, 1070, 21)

Tamayo's complete lack of sympathy for all the scoundrels of the nineteenth century, the men of high society and government, may have cost him the fame of being one of Spain's first-rank playwrights. Had he suppressed his moral indignation, lessened his preaching, and stayed closer to the aesthetic aspects of his art, he might have produced several plays like *Un drama nuevo* (*A New Drama*). But again, had he done this he would not have been Tamayo.[25]

VII   Del dicho al hecho (Actions Speak Louder).
Tamayo and Nature

Actions Speak Louder, which overflows with sentiment, is perhaps the least admirable of Tamayo's dramas. Nevertheless, it tells the reader a great deal about his attitude towards nature and art. In addition to the various ideas and images that often appear in Tamayo's plays (for example, the orphan girl, the scorn of court and praise of village,[26] the "money does not bring happiness," and the "be charitable to the poor") there are two more that open a new vista. These two additional ideas concern Tamayo's attitude towards nature and sex.

In *Actions Speak Louder,* the cruel Leandro kills a dog named Leal (Loyal, in English), who belongs to his lifelong friend, Thomas. The amount of sentiment spent on this episode passes belief, especially when one considers that its author was thirty-four years of age.

The Leal episode opens the reader's eyes to something important. Reflecting on this sentimentalized canine, he realizes that Tamayo in his plays rarely alludes to nature or its creatures. Indeed, Tamayo never seems to mention any animals, plants, mountains, rivers, streams, gardens, flowers, days of sunshine, dawn, sunset, fog, mist—anything that has to do with nature—as if the events in his plays stood aside from nature and took place in a vacuum ruled over by eschatology. Tamayo sees everything *sub specie aeternitatis,* so much so that he strips nature of its beauty and warmth and even destroys it. For human beings, eternity is a kind of void that staggers the mind. Tamayo tends towards finality: he sees the forest but not the trees, and when he does decide to single out a tree (in this case the dog, Leal) it is not a tree or a dog at all. It is an animal deprived of animal flesh and blood. It is an animal as Tamayo's momentary sentiment would have him believe an animal to be.

It has been said that the supernatural takes up where the natural leaves off, or that it redeems the natural. In Tamayo, the supernatural swallows up the natural and destroys it.[27]

Another example of this destruction is Tamayo's attitude towards sex. In his plays a man loves a woman's soul or Womanhood or something of the sort; he never loves one of those *serranas* (mountain lasses) of the Marqués de Santillana (1398-1458), the Isabel Freyre of Garcilaso de la Vega (1503-1536), the amazingly beautiful young girls of Cervantes' short novels (*ca.* 1613), the hauntingly beautiful women of Bécquer (1836-1870), or the girls with red lips of Manuel Machado (1874-1947). Here are Thomas' words to Gabriela, from *Actions Speak Louder;* he loves her, but she does not know it:

Well, yes; I am in love with a girl prettier than a rose[28] and better than bread; not in a way I see some others fall in love but in a very different way, I don't even dare look at her. I am tempted at times—may God pardon me—to commend myself to her as to a saint. (*OC*, 892, 28)

Although sanctity is unquestionably a desirable goal, one wonders if young men fall in love with young girls merely because they are saints, or if it is wholesome that they do so. It does not seem natural.

VIII   *Tamayo and* Admiratio

Actions Speak Louder also contains some extraordinary episodes, the most marvelous of which is Leandro's sudden inheritance of eight million *reales* from a man he scarcely knew. This amazing fortune brings to mind the several millions Rafael inherited from his friend, Edward, in *The Right Track*. The key adjectives are "marvelous," "sudden," and "amazing," which are descriptive of the many happy endings, religious conversions, and abrupt changes of characters in Tamayo's plays. How does one account for all this?

There is in art a principle known as *admiratio*,[29] which may be translated as amazement or wonderment. It is the awe a person experiences on witnessing something unusual or exciting. The *admiratio* may perhaps result from something sensational at a circus, or from a soliloquy of Hamlet or Segismundo; it is apparent that *admiratio* has varying degrees of profundity or dignity. In literature, the reader's wonderment may come not only from what is said, but from the manner of saying it; wonderment in Cervantes' *Exemplary Novels*, for instance, will arise both from the marvelous argument of each story and from the author's mastery of the Spanish language. The reader will experience an unusual delight, and at the same time he can profit from the example.

Apparently Tamayo and his contemporaries felt that an unexpected and startling event in a play (let it be called "Suddenness in the theater") produces a proper wonderment. Thus men can inherit vast fortunes between the acts of a drama, and villains can quickly change their evil ways and become devotees of the Lord. The majority of theatergoers in the mid-nineteenth century must have felt the same way, because even a play as poor as *Actions Speak Louder* was successful. Large doses of sentiment caused wonderment, and that, after all, seemed to be the desideratum. To the reader of our time, this kind of wonderment often seems banal.[30]

There is no need for our own astonishment at Tamayo's fault on the score of *admiratio*. And apologies for his lapse from decorum would seem to be misplaced. He was as he was, and it is our privilege to try to understand him in the same way his own contemporaries understood him.

IX No hay mal que por bien no venga
(Every Evil Hath Its Good)

Tamayo may always be remembered as the playwright who wrote good plays and then ruined them in the third act. There is no better example of this than *Every Evil Hath Its Good*.

The first two acts are a delightful comedy. The forty-year-old *calavera* (playboy), Enrique, has invited a young friend, Julián Benavides, to stay with him. Julián's book, *Women in the Light of Philosophy*, is a best seller that preaches the liberation of women. The two men have humorous arguments over this question since Enrique, in spite of his loose conduct, has old-fashioned ideas.

The comedy is based on what Henri Bergson[31] has called "mechanical rigidity" (which takes place, for example, when a pompous man slips and falls on the ice, or when Sancho Panza trembles at the sight of a squire with a huge nose). Enrique, the middle-aged playboy who professes to be a Christian, is really an awkward straw man, a clown, sparring with his younger atheistic friend, Julián. The latter, on the other hand, is a wooden puppet clumsily trying to parry the blows of his older companion and making counterblows. Their actions are directed to what Bergson calls the pure intelligence rather than the sentiments,[32] and the heart is not involved. Thus an audience, no matter what its religious preference, can laugh at their stupidity.

The comedy grows with the appearance of Luisa, Enrique's daughter, who has run away from her boarding school. She has been reading *Women in the Light of Philosophy* which, unknown to her, is Julián's book, and she feels that she is liberated, a modern young woman. She is very forward with Julián and this infuriates Enrique, who expects more modesty in his daughter.

In the meantime, the irate father of a woman Enrique has wronged comes to see him. The father's recriminations can be heard offstage. Luisa, who has really fallen in love with Julián, thinks he is the one who has wronged the woman and now she strives to keep him at arm's length. This awkward sparring of the two young lovers adds to that Bergsonian mechanical rigidity which is the source of the ridiculous.

After the first two acts, the reader is prepared to say: "a most delightful comedy." But the third act is a clumsy volte-face. Casting aside the appeal to intelligence, Tamayo suffuses everything with sentiment. Enrique has become a moralizer, a cloying *raisonneur*. He, the Christian, must now humble Julián the Atheist, whose submission is abject. If Tamayo had lived in a different century, he might not have destroyed his fun with his morality.

X   Los hombres de bien (The Upright Men)

Having written his masterpiece, *A New Drama*, in 1867, it seems unlikely that Tamayo could have returned to the moral posturing of his earlier plays, but he did just that in *Every Evil Hath Its Good* (1868) and *The Upright Men* (1870). In fact, in *The Upright Men*, the last play from his pen, he arrived at almost unadulterated moralization. The title of the play is ironical, for the "upright men" are really hypocrites. They are concerned only with their own well-being. They are upright in name only. They are cowards who back down in the face of danger, taking a bit of snuff as they do so.

The plot of the play pits evil, in the person of the foul Leandro Quiroga, against good, which is apparently represented by the upright men but really represented by the humble country lad, Damián Ortiz, and the girl Andrea, who lives in a hut with her old father. These good people have no money.

Quiroga has come to the country to lust after Andrea and another girl, Adelaida, the daughter of a wealthy gentleman. This gentleman and his friends, who are also wealthy, are the "upright men." They constantly talk of virtue and they look good in society, but when it comes to removing Quiroga from the scene, they make excuses in their hypocritical way. Damián, however, tries to help the two young women against the lustful Quiroga. Andrea needs his support because she is socially helpless, although she has great inner strength and virtue. Adelaida also needs his support, because she is weak inside, although she does have social strength and position. Adelaida has been educated in modern ways.

Damián, the *raisonneur,* often makes a speech like the following:

Yes, you are unhappy. It is fate, you say? No. The grief and ignominy you now weep over are the fruit of pride. Of pride, Adelaida, which seems to make one ascend by the very zeal and pangs it brings one down with. Humility is just the opposite: with it we seem to go down when we are really ascending. Be humble, and you can rise from the abyss you now find yourself sunk in; be proud, and you will find yourself sunk even more in the mud. A great ignominy will quickly grow from a great vanity. (*OC*, 1120, 18)

One brief speech of Damián sums up the style and much of the content of the play. Quiroga and an accomplice have come to carry off Andrea against her will, and Damián cries out after them:

Andrea! (*He is desperate, calling her.*) Unhappy girl! The hawks are carrying off the dove! (*Weeping.*) (*OC*, 1130, 10)

As observed above, *The Upright Men* is a play about evil and good, about predatory men and dovelike creatures.

Excessive moralization in the theater brings an abundance of sentiment. Damián is lame and walks with a limp, an affliction

that is supposed to evoke sympathy in the breast of the audience.
He also has a dog named Leal, the same kind of unnatural canine
that appeared in *Actions Speak Louder,* and once again this
animal, the sign of goodness, is treacherously slain. And the
audience can sympathize with Adelaida, the poor rich girl, the
weak woman who is seduced by the evil Quiroga and runs
off with him: Adelaida never knew her mother!

The Upright Men is the only one of Tamayo's moral plays
without a happy ending. Although things turn out well for Andrea
and Damián, Quiroga and Adelaida are not converted at the end.
It would seem that for Tamayo and his dramatic characters, the
politico-religious lines between traditionalists and liberals had
hardened by 1870 and become a stone wall. In this, the year of
his final salute to the theater, not even stage villains could cross
the no-man's-land. Adelaida, the young woman who was
educated in the English fashion (*Las señoritas que nos hemos
educado a la inglesa,* OC, 1117, 20), has been reading Renan's
book, *The Life of Jesus,*[33] which denies the divinity of Jesus
Christ. On the other hand, Damián, Tamayo's spokesman, has
been reading the catechism:

DAMIÁN. That's the result of my studying nothing about politics since
     I learned the Catechism of Ripalda in school. (*OC,* 1111,
     16)[34]

In 1870, the year of "Spain Without a King,"[35] the year in
which the first Vatican Council pronounced the doctrine of
Papal Infallibility, there could be no happy ending between the
Renanists and the faithful disciple of the Catechism of Ripalda,
Don Manuel Tamayo y Baus.[36]

XI   *The Moral Plays: Conclusions*

The poor man and the son of pride were the favorite
characters of Tamayo. His poor man is apt to be an orphan with
a physical defect, or he may have a dog named Leal. He is a
creature of sentiment who sees everything *sub specie aeternitatis.*
Other men may make millions, Tamayo's poor man cares not.
Other men may own banks and railroads and factories, let them

own them, for they will not find happiness in this "delusive worth."[37] The rich may hoard their wealth, no matter; if he the poor man inherits a fortune, he will give it to the poor and marry the defenseless girl being victimized by a son of pride. Like Damián in *The Upright Men,* he will save his soul and the soul of all those who choose to profit by his example. This question of choice is important, for Tamayo is an advocate of free will.[38]

In creating his poor man, Tamayo sometimes confuses poverty of spirit with mere poverty. The former implies a detachment from the things of this world in the fashion of Thomas More or Francisco Borja, it does not necessarily mean that a man will not possess the things of this world. But Tamayo's moral plays display no attempt at refinement of meaning. They equate money, which leads to worldly attachment, with unhappiness and even with evil.

Tamayo's son of pride has a fixation as strong as that of the poor man, at least until the end of any play in which he appears. For the sake of his god, money, he forgets the example of his sainted mother, he abandons his friends, he turns his back on his childhood sweetheart, he ignores all that is good and holy, until the last scene when, overcome by a *deus ex machina* conversion, he admits his total fault and the wisdom of his opponent. He stands erect now on "the rugged road" and directs his thoughts to his eternal dwelling place.[39]

Tamayo's moral plays, written in the 1860's, reflect the tone of the letter he wrote to the Carlists in 1871. Good is good and evil is evil; there are no gradations between them. According to his aesthetics, the theater imitates real life. In real life, as it is described in the Carlist letter,[40] Liberalism brings "*horrendous* evils," "*brutal* force," "*scandalous* success," and "*perpetual* war." By imitation, in the theater, the new rich Liberals are "*insolent* millionaires" displaying "*base* vanity" and an "*infamous* thirst for gold." They have, moreover, a monstrous newspaper with "*countless* tongues." The way out of all these evils is to see that "God's will be done" in "the holy joys of the family." Tamayo's moral dramas show the same extreme use of adjectives as the Carlist letter because their basic meaning is the same. Tamayo the moralizer, Tamayo the faithful son of the old order, is protesting modern innovation.

XII *The* Alta Comedia

The moral plays of Tamayo and his contemporaries were generally labeled *alta comedia* or "high comedy,"[41] an expression that pertains both to their meaning and their form. They are "high comedy" because they concern the upper middle class; they are also "high comedy" because their language was thought to be superior to the exuberant language of the Romantic playwrights.

In theory, dramas of this kind will have all or most of the following characteristics: written mostly during the years 1845-1870, they concern a contemporary problem taken from high society; their language is sober[42] and eloquent; they insist on a certain decorum, known as *buen tono*; they propose an ideal, for example, Tamayo's "God, King and Country"; they have a complicated plot and may use the *deus ex machina* to resolve the intrigue; they see the libertine and wealthy businessman as the enemies of society; they create a *raisonneur* to oppose these enemies; they do not have the grand passions of the Romantic school, by which a man like Don Álvaro[43] hurls himself off a cliff with satanic grin—they present the more common passions arising over conflicts such as "marriage for love or money." Above all, they are didactic.

At first glance, the *alta comedia* may seem close to reality, closer, say, than the plays of the Romantics, but its realism will not stand close scrutiny. The happy endings and sudden conversions take precedence over the problems and activities of everyday life. They are unreal. Nevertheless, the Madrid middle class loved this sort of play and packed the theaters to see it. Tamayo and his fellow playwright, Adelardo López de Ayala (1828-1879), were the idols of their day.

XIII *The Historical Background of Tamayo's Moral Plays*

Tamayo's indignation in his high comedy was largely provoked by the economic expansion of the nineteenth century, which he found unwelcome. In 1837 laws were passed by which the Church was to give up its lands to the small farmer and the Public Treasury, but in effect they often went to wealthy men who fattened on these new gains. The mining industry grew rapidly between 1839 and 1868, when Europe looked to Spain for bituminous coal, lead, and copper. There was a new impetus for naval construction. The most extraordinary development came in the textile industry where the mechanical loom and steamboat transportation forced many small factories to close; there were now large plants employing many more workers. One statistic will underscore this economic change: the investment in textiles rose from 414 million *reales* in 1842 to a billion or more in 1860.[44]

The textile industrialists were true to their Liberal credo in everything except free trade, where out of self-interest they favored a protective tariff rather than open exchange with foreign countries. Thus they were inconsistent in their Liberalism and shamelessly money-minded. To a man like Tamayo, always firm in his principles, they must have seemed hypocritical. Did it not follow that Liberalism was systematic hypocrisy? The author of the Carlist letter, which speaks in terms of good and evil, would answer, *yes.*

One result of the economic expansion was the affluent society of 1856-1866 with its *haute bourgeoisie.*[46] This society opened the door to many things deplorable to a traditionalist: the easy establishment of newspapers,[46] the railway boom, prompted in part by French (foreign!) capital, the sudden building of new roads, the acceptance of the banker as a respected figure in society, the bourgeois speculator and rack-renter,[47] the sale of municipal commons, numerous financial scandals, the vulgar ostentation of the new rich, and the growth of imported luxury from France. These things were anathema to a man of Tamayo's temperament. He could no more accept them than accept Ernest Renan's scandalous book of 1863, *The Life of Jesus,* which denied the divinity of Jesus of Nazareth. Everything he stood for—as a Catholic, as a Carlist, and a gentleman—was under attack, as if some intelligent Adversary were directing the entire operation.

This is not to say that Tamayo's hurt and disenchantment were entirely subjective. Even a man with whom Tamayo had little in common, Francisco Pi y Margall, was disillusioned by the conduct of his countrymen. In his book, *La República de 1873,* he wrote:

My bitter experiences in power have been so great that I no longer desire it. I have lost in Government my tranquility, my repose, my illusions, my confidence in men, which constituted the foundation of my character. For every loyal man, I have found ten traitors; for every grateful man, a hundred ingrates; for every selfless and patriotic man, a hundred who only sought in politics the stuffing of their appetites.[48]

If Pi y Margall, the heterodox honest man, could write in this fashion about the men of his time, it is little wonder that Tamayo, the orthodox honest man, whose traditional beliefs were under fire, looked upon them as candidates for hell.

Tamayo did not have to look far for living examples of the money lust he scorned in his plays. Speculators appeared on all sides, and one of them, José de Salamanca (1811-1883), was the most famous figure of his day. This Andalusian lawyer three times made and lost fortunes valued at hundreds of millions of *reales*.[49] He gained control of the salt monopoly, constructed railroads in Spain, Italy, Portugal, and the Danubian countries, and built a luxurious suburb near Madrid.

With his money, Salamanca gathered a select library,[50] although he himself had problems with simple spelling: he dropped his *h*'s, confused his *b*'s and *v*'s and *ll*'s and *y*'s, and did not know the use of accent marks, periods, and commas. He built a sumptuous palace and stocked it with priceless paintings, for others to admire. He had part of a railroad track laid in silver. He encouraged French cuisine in his palace and favored one ballerina, a French blonde, *la Guy*, over another ballerina, an Italian brunette, *la Fuoco* who was favored by his enemy, General Narváez. He founded or subsidized newspapers to combat Narváez. He built a magnificent theater. He had huge stables of horses. He sired several illegitimate children. To a man like Tamayo, who saw everything in terms of the life to come, Salamanca must have been a totally repugnant character. It is fair to conclude that he and other negotiators like him were the models of the *haute bourgeoisie* in Tamayo's moral dramas ("insolent millionaires," "vile action," "the newspaper . . . monster of countless tongues").

One historian, commenting on Salamanca's Madrid-Aranjuez railroad of 1851, has said:

It was the sign of the profound transformation beginning to operate in the rhythm of Spanish life, and the people were not aware of its transcendent meaning.[51]

Tamayo was a Spanish gentleman accustomed to the old rhythm of Spanish life. He was naïve and unaware of economic theory. His spontaneous reaction to "the profound transformation beginning to operate in the rhythm of Spanish life" was his moral theater. Thus, paradoxically, the so-called high comedy is more like an instinctive comedy, a "low" comedy, where reason plays a secondary role. It is based on Tamayo's sentiments.[52]

CHAPTER 3

Tamayo Entertains

I *Introduction*

TAMAYO, who admired the dramas of Shakespeare, must have known the lines of Sir Toby and the clown from *Twelfth Night*:

SIR TOBY. Dost thou think, because thou art virtuous, there shall be
  no more cakes and ale?
CLOWN. Yes, by Ste Anne; and ginger shall be hot i' the mouth too.

Tamayo may have suppressed the truth of these lines in his moral plays, but not everything in his theater is virtue, religion, and salvation. There is another side of it that aims at cakes and ale, at entertainment. This side includes short humorous pieces, a melodramatic imitation of Schiller, a tragedy, three historical dramas, a play about jealousy, and a drama about actors who act out the roles of a play-within-the-play. The present chapter will consider the short humorous pieces and the melodramatic imitation of Schiller; in all these plays the action and plot predominate over characterization.[1] The other works mentioned above will be treated in subsequent chapters.[2]

II *The One-Act Plays*

At the beginning of his career, Tamayo wrote two one-act plays, *Una apuesta* (*A Wager*) and *Huyendo del perejil* (*Out of the Frying Pan*). Although he had a special talent for these shorter works, he stopped writing them until the last years of his career, when he wrote one more *Más vale maña que fuerza* (*Better Cunning Than Force*).

The first of the short works, *A Wager* (1851), was an original play suggested by the eighteenth-century French *La Gageure*

Imprévue.[3] *A Wager* tells the amusing love story of Félix and Clara.

The widow Doña Clara is talking with her servant Julia about a lawsuit she has undertaken and also about the man who lives next door. She finds him attractive. One day she deliberately drops her book out the window and the man, Don Félix, retrieves it. Both Félix and Clara talk formally to each other, but he knows how to flatter her and wagers ten gold ounces with her that within twenty-four hours he can make her fall in love with him. She accepts the wager and grants him three visits within the allotted time. In a soliloquy, Clara declares that Félix is a man whom a lady might indeed love. Félix meantime tells Julia she must always speak badly of him in Clara's presence. Félix tells Clara that she alone reigns in his heart, which delights her, and later she gets very annoyed when Julia speaks against him. Clara is bewildered now since she does not want to lose the wager, but knows she cannot win it. Félix sees to it that her lawsuit turns out well. At the end, when he teasingly says he has fears about winning the wager, Clara directs herself to the audience and beseeches it to calm Félix' fears: "a woman beseeches you," she says. This insight into feminine psychology gives the play a delightful touch.

The success of *A Wager* depends on the smooth flow of the dialogue and the ability of Tamayo to move his three characters, Félix, Clara, and Julia, on and off stage. He accomplishes both with remarkable ease, and the reader is willing to accept his contrived plot. *A Wager* provides a little "ginger, hot i' the mouth."

III   Huyendo del perejil (Out of the Frying Pan), *1853*

One Spanish refrain for "out of the frying pan into the fire" is *huyendo del perejil, le nació en la frente,* which provided the title for Tamayo's one-act *Out of the Frying Pan.*

The play tells the story of young Rafael, who has fallen in love with a poor girl and secretly married her. His widower father, the Marquis, is furious and hopes to dissolve the marriage. Rafael insists that his bride is beautiful, good, and discreet, but his father will hear none of it.

One day Rafael and his father are travelling through the country and their coach breaks down. While waiting to have it fixed, they stay at the home of a young lady, Carolina, who is very gracious and hospitable. The father falls in love with her and asks her to marry him.

It turns out that Carolina is really Rafael's bride; the young couple has arranged the coach's breakdown in order to convince the Marquis that a young man can be swept off his feet by a beautiful young lady. Finally, the Marquis has to give in, and he approves of their marriage.

Both *Out of the Frying Pan* and *A Wager* provide rapid movement and wittily pleasing dialogue. In both cases, the audience is willing to accept Tamayo's contrived plots.

IV   Más vale maña que fuerza
(Better Cunning Than Force), *1866*

This humorous one-act play was written some thirteen years after the others.

Two young married men, Antonio and Miguel, are thinking of going to a masked ball. Their wives, Elisa and Juana, do not take to the idea and set about keeping their husbands home, but in different ways. Elisa is kindly and affectionate towards Antonio and even urges him to go, whereas Juana, the vixen, hounds her husband into desperation. At the end, Antonio stays home and a harassed Miguel runs off to the ball. As Elisa says, "wives who want to control their husbands should use cunning rather than force."

In the third scene, Juana plays on the male pride and fears of Elisa's husband, Antonio. Their dialogue is perhaps the most humorous Tamayo ever penned.

According to a note on the title page of *Better Cunning Than Force*, "this play is an imitation of the French comedy *La Diplomatie du Ménage*, which opened in Paris in 1852." The word "imitation" should be construed to mean "only the same plot." Tamayo radically changed the French original by introducing more lively dialogue and by changing one of the four characters from a servant to a husband, Miguel, the comic victim of a hectoring wife (the classic *mujer brava*).[4] The comic force of Tamayo's play makes it an original creation.

V Ángela. An *"Imitation"* of Schiller's
Love and Intrigue, 1852

The English novelist Graham Greene has written several books he calls "entertainments," to distinguish them from his other novels. An entertainment tells a story with a lot of action, and its plot has secret schemes or international conspiracies. It is the sort of narrative that popular movies are made of, for it makes an audience forget the cares of the day. It has no transcendent meaning.[5]

Tamayo's *Ángela* might also be classified as an entertainment. The action takes place in an Italian ducal court about the year 1770. The unscrupulous Grand Chamberlain, San Mario, plans to marry his son Conrado to the scandalous countess, Adelaida, in order to secure his own position. Conrado, however, refuses to submit to his father's will since he is in love with Ángela, a young commoner who earns her living making artificial flowers.

San Mario is furious, and he plans to change Conrado's mind by ruining Ángela's reputation. Through the services of an evil friend, Araldi, he lets an old marquis into Ángela's house via a secret door. The young girl defies the marquis, but she must hide him when Conrado pays her a visit. Conrado, however, discovers him. In the next scene, these three are joined by San Mario and Ángela's mother. Since Conrado continues to defy his father out of love for Ángela, he must go to jail.

In the meantime, an old man tells Ángela that the evil Grand Chamberlain is not Conrado's real father. As a result, she goes to have a heart-to-heart talk with Countess Adelaida who, persuaded by the girl's virtue, promises to reform her lascivious ways and to protect her. But things take a turn for the worse. San Mario forces Ángela to write a love letter to the old marquis, an incorrigible *viejo verde,* by threatening to kill her mother. Ángela tells San Mario she knows he is not Conrado's father. Conrado comes into possession of the love letter that Ángela wrote under duress.

The entanglement grows in Act IV and culminates in the ball,
where the marquis and countess learn they are exiled, an apparently mad Ángela seeks justice, and Conrado, also apparently
mad, declares that San Mario is not his father. The duke (who
never appears in the play) has ordered San Mario's arrest.

Meantime, San Mario's evil friend, Araldi, has prepared a
venomous potion for Ángela to drink, but San Mario mistakenly
takes it. At the end, with all the characters present, San Mario
dies, and the last obstacle to the young couple's happy future
has been removed.[6]

This story is merely an entertainment, and the reader can
visualize its conversion into a movie or television drama with
his preferred actors cast as the villainous San Mario and the
young lovers.

VI *Schiller*

The readers of the German poet, Johann Friedrich Schiller,
will recognize in *Ángela* the plot of *Kabale und Liebe* (*Love and
Intrigue*), 1784. San Mario takes the place of Chancellor von
Walter, Conrado is his son Ferdinand von Walter, Ángela is
Luise Miller, Countess Adelaida is Lady Milford, and Araldi is
the evil Wurm. Ángela's ineffective mother is a weak substitute
for Luise's father, Miller, who has a principal role in Schiller's
drama.

Tamayo made no secret of his debt to Schiller. In the long
prologue he wrote to *Ángela*, he states:

The present drama is the legitimate offspring of *Love and Intrigue*
of Schiller: it resembles this play like a son does a father; it has the
family air. It is, however, an essentially different being, with another
form, another heart, a distinct soul. Like the spark that issues forth
from flint struck by steel, this drama has issued from my fantasy
struck by the impression caused in it by the reading of the work of
my illustrious and esteemed master, J. C. Federico Schiller.

Noble hearts must acknowledge debts of gratitude and mine
would be base if it failed to recognize what it owes to the great
poet, the pride and glory of Germany today . . .

I give the name of original to my work because I cannot think
of another name more fitting. In it there are three situations and

four or five thoughts similar to those of the German drama . . .[7]
(*OC*, 150-51)

Schiller's *Love and Intrigue* is one of the most famous dramas
of the western stage. It has a historical inspiration in the court
of Karl Eugen, Duke of Württemberg, where Schiller went to
school and came under the personal rule of that despot. It throws
light on "the august foundations of the social order,"[8] and is
considered to be the best bourgeois tragedy of German literature. In its development of the social-amorous conflict that arises
when the noble Ferdinand falls in love with the bourgeoise
Luise, the reader comes across many memorable lines:

. . . when we burst this hateful husk of class . . .[9]

True I am of noble birth. Let us see if my title is more ancient
than the universe's primeval plan, my escutcheon more worthy than
the words heaven has writ in Luise's eyes: "This woman is for
this man."[10]

Schiller's play deserves inclusion in any theater's repertory.
It can be seen over and over again. Its speeches can be learned
by heart. Tamayo's *Ángela*, on the other hand, is to be seen once
as a source of pleasure in the theater. When he says his play is
an "imitation" of Schiller, Tamayo means a free adaptation of
Schiller's plot and an original entertainment, for he has made no
effort to capture the profound significance of the German
drama.[11]

CHAPTER 4

The Tragedy Virginia and the Historical Dramas

I Virginia A *Tragedy in Five Acts,* 1853

IT occasionally happens in literature that an author favors one
of his works over all the others, even though it is the others
to which he owes his fame. He has, as it were, a favorite child
who has the right of primogeniture, and the rest of his children
are second sons. This was the case with Tamayo, who staged
the tragedy *Virginia* when he was twenty-four years old. He
always admired this drama, which he once called "my greatest
delight and cruelest hardship, the almost exclusive sustenance
of my soul,"[1] and later in life, when he no longer invented
new plays for the theater, he rewrote *Virginia* again and again
until he finally left a second version of it. His other offspring
left his house and board, so to speak, but *Virginia* always re-
mained by his side.

Many authors had written a *Virginia* before Tamayo: Mariet,
Dutheil, Leclerc, Chabanon, Le Blanc, Campistron, La Harpe,
and Latour de Saint-Ibars in France; Alfieri in Italy; Count Leopold in Sweden; and Juan de la Cueva, Montiano, and Ledesma
in Spain. Tamayo explicitly mentions all these authors in a
letter to his friend Manuel Cañete, and he says that he has
read five of them. He admires the dramas of Alfieri, Latour de
Saint-Ibars, and Count Leopold, but he holds those of Montiano
and Ledesma in little esteem. Apparently he did not read the
Virginia of his well-known countryman, Juan de la Cueva (1560?-
1610?).[2]

II *The Source of* Virginia

The story of *Virginia* comes from the pages of the Roman historian, Livy, whose account of the crime of Appius Claudius

and the sacrifice of Virginia by her father, Virginius, has been the source of all the *Virginia* plays. It is a dramatic story indeed.

In Rome, the magistrate Appius Claudius is burning with love for the beautiful daughter of Lucius Virginius, who is absent from the city on an army campaign. Virginia is betrothed to Lucius Icilius, a tribune and defender of the people's cause. Appius fails to win Virginia by promises and gifts, and so he conceives an evil scheme. He tells his servant, Marcus Claudius, to bring up a false lawsuit, to swear in court that Virginia's mother was his slave and that she, the slave's daughter, belongs to him. He will back up Marcus Claudius' demands, and in the absence of the girl's father there should be no trouble.

One day Appius' servant apprehends Virginia in the plaza, but a crowd convenes to defend her and the honor of her family. Then the servant says that he does not want her by force, but only after a court trial before the magistrate, who will decide his case. The crowd and Virginia then go to appear before Appius. Appius declares that he wants the father to come forth and that until he does the claimant will have possession of Virginia. The crowd is annoyed at this but does not dare to object openly, upon which Virginia's grandfather and Icilius, her betrothed, come to protect her. Icilius defies Appius and says he will defend Virginia with steel: "the betrothed of Icilius will not remain outside her father's house." Appius sees that Icilius has moved the crowd and decides to let Virginia go free for another day. The relatives then send for her father, Virginius, in the field. Appius sends letters ordering the arrest of Virginius, but they arrive too late, for he is on his way to Rome.

On the day of the trial, Virginius, dressed in mourning, appears in the forum with his daughter. The entire city is there. Virginius warns the crowd that the same plight may one day be theirs; if it can happen to a soldier in the field it can also happen to them. But Appius' will prevails. His mind crazed by illicit love, he passes sentence on Virginia without even hearing the arguments of the claimant or her father. She is to be the slave of Marcus Claudius. Everyone is frightened by this abominable act. The crowd objects and Virginius tries to arouse it, but Appius' menacing words cow the people, who step back and leave Virginia alone in the forum.

Virginius speaks politely to Appius and asks him if he can talk to Virginia's nurse to learn of her early childhood. He has been called her father, wrongly it would seem, and he wants to learn the truth of the matter. Appius agrees to his request. Virginius takes his daughter and her nurse aside, near the temple called Cloacina. He draws a knife and tells Virginia that this is the only way he can preserve her liberty. He plunges the knife into her breast.

Appius orders the arrest of Virginius, but the latter gets away in the midst of the protective crowd. Icilius, Virginia's betrothed, and her grandfather take the girl's body and show it to the people, who all curse Appius' wickedness and weep over the lost beauty and the distress of her father. The matrons ask: is that what comes of raising children, or is this the reward of chastity? And the crowd, says Livy, was disturbed.

III   *Tamayo's* Virginia

Virginio,[3] Icilio, and the tribune Aulo open Tamayo's play with a formal discussion of home and country; the hendeca-syllables[4] of the first act add to the gravity of their argument. If a man has a good wife, the mother of a family, and Rome, the mother of all, he has everything. Virginio and Icilio are themselves examples of the model Roman: the former is a devoted father and soldier who will risk his life against Rome's enemies; the latter, betrothed to the chaste Virginia, is a tribune who defends the people.

But there are clouds on the horizon, and an augury of a dark future. The magistrates have killed the beloved veteran, Dentato, by having his own men turn on him in battle. Rome is now menaced from without and from within.

The scene shifts to the wedding of Virginia and Icilio, which follows the rite of the god Hymen. The externals of the cere-mony are Roman—the torches, the ritual use of water and fire, and the special torch of Hymen—but Tamayo's theme is one of the classic themes of Spanish literature, *La perfecta casada* (*The Perfect Wife*) of Fray Luis de León (1527-1591). Virginio is speaking to Virginia:

... the married woman shines in the depth of her tranquil hearth more than in the sun's own rays. Always intact let her honor gleam, and if in peril she sometimes finds herself, she resists, she fights, she overcomes, or emits her dying breath.

If the nuptial couch yields flowers, let them find in you the tree that gives them shade. (*OC*, 271, 27-34)

The phrase "emits her dying breath" recalls the story of the Roman lady and martyr, Lucretia, à precursor of *la perfecta casada* in the pre-Christian era (6th century B.C.). This is the first suggestion, or presentiment, of Virginia's fate. A second presentiment appears later in the words of her old nurse, Camila, who wonders why on this happy day her breast is the battle-ground of both joy and sorrow.

After the wedding, the magistrate Apio Claudio comes to announce the presence of enemy troops. The men gladly depart in defense of Rome and leave their women behind. Claudio then briefly describes his lust to his servant, Marco.

In the second act Claudio comes to Virginia's house to profess his love, but she rejects him. The action moves rapidly now; Icilio returns from the field to protect his spouse and both he and Aulo defy Claudio in Virginia's house and make him leave. Tamayo's style at times is sententious:

CLAUDIO. A woman's heart is made of wax. Yours will soften, I know.
VIRGINIA. The heart of a Roman wife is wax to virtue, to wicked-
        ness steel.

The style also displays, at times, the same extreme character it had in his letter to his Carlist constituents (see Chapter 1); the virtuous are very virtuous and the vicious very vicious; neither seem to falter. Claudio is "the ferocious monster who consumes his victims' tears"; he is a "perfidious monster"; and Icilio refers to "the wantonness of his nefarious vices." Virginia, on the other hand, is a "rare prodigy of innocence and beauty."

The various presentiments of doom reach their climax at the middle of the play, when Virginia describes her troubled dream:

Oh that sleep had never overcome me! I slept. I dreamed! Fateful visions crossed the shades in silence, when in the onslaught of the

fierce hurricane with thunder and lightning exploding Claudio of a
sudden appears: he sees me, his eyes shine with sinister light; I
want to shout, and in my throat the voice dies mute, and the frightful
specter runs towards me. . . . But in that very instant, in haste from
the clouds descending, a woman thrusts herself between us, a bloody
dagger fixed in her heart. Claudio sees her and trembles and with-
draws and she, subduing his neck with her foot, cries out: "I am
Lucretia. Another tyrant wrenched from me my joy and honor;
dying I laved my stain and drowned the impious tyrant in the blood
that poured from my breast."

. . . .

And Lucretia fixing her stare on me said: "The country groans
beneath new infamy: may another woman's blood cleanse it; I await
you." And she took flight. And the deep thunder in its last complaint
"I await you" clamors in lugubrious sound. And the hurricane disap-
pearing in the sphere with dolorous *ay*! repeated, "I await you."
(*OC*, 288-89)

Tamayo, even when evoking a heroine of pre-Christian antiquity,
is never far removed from Christian thought. Lucretia, subduing Claudio with her foot on his throat, is apparently meant to
recall the icon of Mary, Queen of Heaven, crushing the ser-
pent's head.

In the remaining scenes of Act III, Tamayo does something
that seems inexplicable, for it throws his drama awry and robs
it of its force. He diminishes the position of Virginia's husband,
Icilio, and exalts her father in such a way that Icilio is made to
look childish and foolish. All the characters are on stage, except
Virginio, who is still in the field. Marco, conspiring with Apio
Claudio, comes to claim Virginia as the daughter of his slave.
Icilio, Virginia, Aulo, and the crowd protest, but Marco insists
on his claim and Claudio comes forward to back him up. The
tyranny of the licentious magistrate has finally come up against
the honor of a Roman family and the passion of the Roman
people; and Icilio, Virginia's husband, is there to protect her.
But instead of letting Icilio protect the honor of his wife, Tamayo
strips him of his dignity and holds the issue aside until the
return of the girl's father, Virginio. The father takes precedence
over the husband. Icilio acts wooden, as if he were the author's
puppet:

ICILIO. (*to the magistrate*): Do you not know that Virginia has a
   father? . . . It is Virginio!
MARCO. A valorous soldier!
AULO. A hero!
ICILIO. Let us await his return!

Perhaps one can explain this dramatic fault by turning to
Tamayo's biography. Barely twenty-four years old when he
staged *Virginia,* he was extremely devoted to the memory of
his late mother, and apparently to his father. Like Icilio, he was
married, and like him also, he was immature and still sought
parental guidance. Thus, he has Icilio act as he himself might
act on a grave occasion.[5]

The fourth act contains the most memorable scene of the
play, in which Apio Claudio summons an augur to foretell the
future. Virginia has called him a Tarquinius, Lucretia's rapist,
and the name of Lucretia has sounded on her lips again and
again. Claudio has spilled the honey he was offering his house-
hold gods, he has torn his toga, he has seen a sinister owl
and a dog, and he wants the augur to interpret these signs. The
augur tells him that his life is fatally linked to that of Virginia;
her death will be his death's announcement. In a soliloquy he
meditates on the words of the augur, but notwithstanding their
dire prophecy, he decides to have Virginia.

In his own house, Apio Claudio confronts Virginia and tells
her his will is law. But she rejects him and dominates the scene:

CLAUDIO. You will not anger me. I love you.
VIRGINIA. Prove it.
CLAUDIO. In what way?
VIRGINIA. Sacrifice is the faithful brother of love. Renounce your
   plan: respect the woman who is loved.
CLAUDIO. Do you wish to die? (*Said as if he remembers the augur's
   prophecy.*)
VIRGINIA. If when loved I live, how can I not love life? Claudio,
   Claudio, why deny yourself the greatest joy that ever en-
   nobled human breast? To dry another's tear. A man's joy
   is fashioned from his neighbor's.

Claudio, carried away by his passion, threatens Virginia; but
she raises a dagger (which appeared in the previous act—Tamayo has prepared his audience) to her breast and cries: "One

step more and you embrace a corpse!" Claudio recalls the augur's sentence and falls to his knees, horrified.

Here again, Tamayo seems to have weakened the force of his drama. Virginio enters and the two men confront each other, as if there were a climax in both the fourth and fifth acts, the first stillborn and the latter closing the play. Claudio gradually regains control of himself and he argues with Virginio. Claudio calls his armed guard, but there is a clamor outside:

MARCO. Sire, the people have risen and storm the gates.

Virginio can now call on the Roman nation.

In the last act, the Roman people gather to the right of the stage. Virginia, Virginio, Icilio, and several women are dressed in mourning, a dress most familiar to the Spanish audience.[6]

Virginio, Virginia, and Icilio beseech the people to help them, but they have been cowed by the armed guard. The magistrate, Claudio, will have his way. The trial takes place, Virginia is judged to be the slave of Marco, the latter refuses to sell her to Virginio, and finally the grieving father asks for permission to address his daughter one last time. He approaches the girl, who understands his intention; he plunges the dagger she gives him into her breast. Icilio cries:

Roman people of Virginia, remember the people of Lucretia.

The aroused crowd struggles with the guard and overcomes it. There are shouts of "Death!" and the crowd converges on Claudio.

IV   The Prologue to Virginia: Tamayo's Theory of Tragedy

On September 8, 1853, three months before Virginia was staged, Tamayo wrote a letter to Manuel Cañete in which he discusses that play and his ideas concerning tragedy. Since then, the letter has been published as the prologue to Virginia.[7]

In the prologue, Tamayo first makes the claim that "the classical tragedy does not live in our literature." There have been recent attempts at tragedy, he says, for example, the dramas of Nicasio Alvarez de Cienfuegos (1764-1809), Gertrudis Gómez de Avellaneda (1814-1873), José Díaz (?-1888), Manuel Quintana (1772-1857), Francisco Martínez de la Rosa (1787-1862), and Joaquín José Cervino (1817-1883), but in spite of the efforts of these authors the tragedy is not flourishing in Spain.[8] He then declares that his own *Virginia* is a tragedy. He is anxious for it to succeed, for if it does not, its failure may strengthen the commonly-held opinion that "tragedy cannot survive on the Spanish scene."

After these introductory remarks, Tamayo gets to the heart of the matter, which is the relation of the modern drama to Greek tragedy. He thinks it is necessary for nineteenth-century authors to break with the Greeks because, great as the Greeks were and beautiful though their dramas may be, "some ancient modes are defects today." One cannot expect a nineteenth-century audience to accept them. He argues against the Greek chorus, which narrows the action, an action already fettered by the unities of time and place. Besides this, there is the question of free will (this doctrine is seldom absent from Tamayo's mind):

In their works the Greeks give an outline of blind instruments of the gods rather than human beings, instruments who, free from struggles within themselves, walk directly to their end, without any obstacle or detention. As a result, with character and sentiment considered to be an effect of fate, they lack a varied and profound development; and the poem in general lacks that moral and philosophical importance which elevates it and makes it the example and instruction of nations.

It is not only the Greek chorus and Greek fate that bind the hands of modern tragedians. Tamayo says the Greeks also employed the three unities, the "triple chain" that the French and Italians later adopted. As a result, the theater of those nations became "affected, mannered and monotonous." In short, the Greek theater is a mold that is not flexible enough for the modern stage. Those dramatists who follow it write unoriginal, monotonous tragedies.[9]

Tamayo then states his case against the Greek theater from the viewpoint of the denouement. In Greek tragedy, everything is a prolonged denouement, an unraveling of the thread, because fate has already ordained what is going to happen. Medea, for example, is always furious and angry with her faithless lover and she plans to have Creon and his promised bride die—without any moral or material obstacle.[10] She never wavers, even though the bride is her own daughter. And later she will plunge the "homicidal steel" into the breast of her own children.

But the public of our day, Tamayo says, first wants a raveling of the thread, a *nouement*, before the unraveling or denouement. It does not want everything set up in advance. It does not want everything to be foretold. That is, it does not want it to be fateful.

The public of our day would want Medea to be not only vengeance; it would want her to be love, sacrifice, disillusion, sorrow, anger, jealousy, wife and mother, and vengeance too, which in the end is triumphant over all.

For Tamayo, "the public of our day" means those Spaniards who are like himself. They are men who experience the industrial changes and agitated life of modern times (the steamboat, the locomotive, the semaphore),[11] but who spiritually live in the sixteenth and seventeenth centuries. Tamayo writes:

And to move the soul and attract the attention of a nineteenth-century audience, will it not be necessary to portray its life, its agitation, its manner of being, that ineffable whole of misery and grandeur . . . ?

Will it not be necessary to break, to pulverize the chains of tradition, and to make tragedy interest and move the audience the same way modern drama does, even though it lose some of its majestic severity? Less insipid simplicity, more logical artifice; less description, more action; less monotonous austerity, more diversity of sounds, more chiaroscuro in the depiction of characters; less head, more soul; less statue, more picture. Such is what the tragedy ought to be, dearest friend,[12] if it is to win citizenship in the Spain of 1853.

Tamayo's argument is an attractive one. Modern society is forever changing. It is always seeking something new, with an insatiable thirst. The tragedian who examines this plight should not be a Greek-like fatalist but a man resembling a Golden Age Spaniard, a Calderón.

But now Tamayo makes a statement that perplexes the reader. He confesses that he is not the nineteenth-century Calderón to do the job!

Are these the changes that I have proposed to introduce in the present work? No, I haven't proposed to introduce a single one of them. An exact governor of my own powers, I have not tried to steer a new course, and only the irresistible urging of my own particular likes and tendencies has prompted me in the present work to mate the modern element somewhat with the ancient.

The reader is tempted to ask: if this is the case, then why write such an attractive prologue for a play that does not live up to the prologue's standards? Indeed, Tamayo seems to agree here with the verdict of one of his critics; namely, his aesthetic theories are far superior to his dramas.[13]

Tamayo's prologue now gives a short lesson in comparative literature, which has been the basis of later comparative studies.[14] Amongst other things, he says that the Spanish Virginias have been "pale and insipid."

V *Schiller*: The Maid of Orleans, *1801; Tamayo*: Juana de Arco (Joan of Arc), *1847*

Tamayo wrote his first play, *Joan of Arc*,[15] when he was eighteen years old. As the subtitle indicates, it is an "Imitation of Schiller."

Both Schiller's play and Tamayo's concern the events of 1424-1431, when the armies of the French King, Charles VII, were being harassed by the English and the Duke of Burgundy. The French were faring very badly, but a young peasant girl, Joan of Arc, came and rallied them at the siege of Orleans. She succeeded in saving the city. After that she became convinced that her mission was to drive the foreigner, the Englishman, out of France. Her efforts were so successful that "before she came, two hundred Englishmen used to drive five hundred Frenchmen before them; after her coming, two hundred Frenchmen could chase five hundred Englishmen."[16] In the end, Joan was captured by the Burgundians and sold to the English, who urged the Inquisition to try her for witchcraft. After a long trial, she was burned at the stake.

Schiller's play takes liberty with the events of history. The seven-year period, 1424-1431, is compressed into what seems like a few days. This compression is important, for Schiller was trying to capture the essence of Joan's mission, an essence that lies outside of time. Tamayo, in imitating his German master, also compresses time.

There are other distortions in both plays, which are of course the privilege of poetic license. The most notable of these is the manner of Joan's death; instead of being burned at the stake, she dies in battle of her wounds. Schiller ended his play this way and the eighteen-year-old Tamayo followed suit.

It is well to discuss Schiller's *Maid of Orleans* before discussing Tamayo's *Joan of Arc*, because in the latter play "imitation" really means "removal." Tamayo took the original edifice and removed certain parts of it.

Schiller's Joan is miraculous. A peasant girl, she alone understands the nature of the war that is destroying France. She alone can defeat the English, but more miraculous than her victory over them is her victory over the Duke of Burgundy. This feudal lord, an ally of the English, hates the French General Duchatel. The man has murdered his father. But the presence of Joan stills the passion in his breast and he embraces Duchatel and accepts him as a brother. Schiller raises the question: What is it that inspires the maiden? Can it be nature, "Joan's secret dialogue with the mountain wind?" Can it be some unknown marvelous power, such as the "brown Bohemian woman" from whom the helmet came? Can it be Joan's asceticism, the fact that she knew "no earthly love?" Or is it the Woman, the Mother of God, who gave Joan a sword to "exterminate my people's woe?"

Schiller is dealing with the unknown, with that region where the visible world leaves off and the invisible world, no less real, takes over. He has no stock answers to the mystery of human existence. Unlike Voltaire,[17] who mocked the metaphysical force of Joan, he respects this and accepts it as a fact. His drama stumbles in the closing scenes, where he cannot comprehend the soul's ascension from the earthly city.[18] Nevertheless, the Woman (the Mother of God) is there to restore order:

JOAN.　See you the rainbow yonder in the air?
　　　　Its golden portals Heaven doth wide unfold,
　　　　Amid the angel choir she radiant stands,
　　　　The eternal Son she claspeth to her breast.

> Her arms she stretcheth forth to me in love.
> How is it with me? Light clouds bear me up—
> My ponderous mail becomes a winged robe;
> I mount—I fly—back rolls the dwindling earth—
> Brief is the sorrow—endless the joy!
> (*Her banner falls, and she sinks lifeless to the ground.*) [19]

Schiller subtitled his *Maid of Orleans* a "Romantic Tragedy." He seemed to be suggesting by these words that reason alone will not account for the mysteries of life. One must make a romantic leap and include the unfathomable message of love, which comes from the will or heart. Joan made that leap, whereas her friends and foes did not. Indeed, they could not. Thus the Catholic Joan of Arc is a source of inspiration to the German Protestant. They are kindred spirits.

VI *Tamayo's* Joan of Arc

It is paradoxical that Tamayo, the Catholic, took an almost naturalistic view of Joan. The invisible forces are gone, the mystery of human existence is gone, except in an occasional address to the Virgin, which Tamayo seems merely to tack on to his play; they are not prayers that issue from the character of Joan. Joan no longer communes with nature, as she does in Schiller's drama, and the helmet is just a helmet, it is not a mysterious object coming from a bizarre gypsy. The duke's conversion, where love overcomes hate, is stated by the author, but it is not felt by the reader. Joan is not miraculous, she does not free herself from the chains, but rather is freed by her father. Joan's love for the English general, Lionel, is briefly suggested in Schiller by her staring into Lionel's face, which robs her of her supernatural virtue, since she has preferred an "earthly love." Tamayo, on the other hand, makes much of Joan's love for Lionel, but this love is not impressive because it does not displace any supernatural ardor. Finally, when Joan dies in Schiller's drama, one senses that heaven is recalling an emissary, a Raphael, a Michael, or, even more, another Virgin. In Tamayo, one simply feels that a practicing Catholic, someone like Tamayo himself, has died, and that Joan will be saved.

VII   *The Difference Between Tamayo and Schiller*

The difference between Schiller's *Maid* and Tamayo's *Joan* can be sensed in an essay Schiller wrote, *On the Use of the Chorus in Tragedy*. Schiller maintains that in tragedy the poet must keep reflection apart from the incidents, and the ideal apart from the sensible (or palpable). He must offer a repose to the action. He must retain his poetical freedom and "inlay and entwine his rigidly contracted plot and the strong outlines of his characters with a tissue of lyrical magnificence, in which, as in flowing robes of purple, they move freely and nobly, with a sustained dignity and exalted repose."[20]

Schiller's *Maid of Orleans* has a "sustained dignity" that is lacking in Tamayo's *Joan of Arc*. The latter play tells its story well, but it does not keep "reflection apart from the incidents." Indeed, there is little reflection. This is not to be wondered at since it was Tamayo's apprentice piece, written when he was eighteen years old.[21]

VIII   La ricahembra (Doña Juana the Magnate), *1854*

In the Spanish language, the word *castizo* means "pure" or "essential," and when applied to literature it refers to those things that are typically Spanish. In this sense, *Doña Juana the Magnate* is *castizo*, the most Spanish of Tamayo's plays. It is not adapted from the French; it is not an imitation of Schiller; it is not a nineteenth-century moral play; it is not a thesis play; it has no counterpart in foreign literature.[22] If it resembles anything, it resembles a *comedia* by the seventeenth-century playwright, Lope de Vega.

Doña Juana the Magnate comes from an episode of medieval history that lies between legend and history. Its source is the manuscript of P. Hernando Pecha, which was finished in 1635. Pecha has this to say of the lady, Doña Juana:

Doña Juana was the oldest daughter of Pero González de Mendoza and Doña Aldonza de Ayala; and in addition to the many outstanding gifts nature gave her, her parents, who had twelve children, so enriched her and bettered her that they called her in Castile *La Ricahembra* (the Lady Magnate). She married Diego Manrique de

Lara, the chief provincial governor of León, who died in the battle of Aljubarrota. And since she was such a perfect woman, and so famous, many great lords attempted to marry her, now that she was a widow. Don Alonso Enríquez, son of Don Fadrique the Maestre de Santiago, was most anxious to make her his wife, and he succeeded in getting his cousin the king Don Juan, who was reigning at the time, to write forcefully to Doña Juana, urging her to marry him. To assure the success of the letter, Don Alonso himself wanted to take it to Doña Juana, disguised as a servant of the king. He went to Guadalajara, where the *Ricahembra* was at the time (she did not know Don Alonso by sight). He asked her for an audience and made his embassy. Doña Juana de Mendoza took the letter and read it, and spoke with annoyance and anger: "Marriages, sir, have to be voluntary. Kings must not do violence in such affairs. Don Alonso is a youth and I of older age, a widow with a child. It does not suit me to marry him, and moreover, I am also moved by other secret reasons and causes." Don Alonso urged Doña Juana to consider the quality of the bridegroom, who was the king's first cousin, the will of the monarch, the benefits she could expect, and other reasons of like kind; he urged Doña so strongly that she became angry and exclaimed: "I don't want to marry the son of a Jewess." Cut by this, Don Alonso raised his hand, slapped Doña Juana, and left. But she, insulted and shamed, said to a servant: "Ask that knight who left here what his name is." The page did so, and Doña Juana did not calm down until Don Alonso came, and also the priest of Santiago, who married them then and there so that no one might ever say that the man who dared to slap her was anyone but her husband. Later the king learned of this story and he praised his deed and hers.[23]

This part of P. Pecha's manuscript constitutes the first act of Tamayo's play.

Tamayo's other three acts tell another story, which also appears in the Pecha manuscript, right after the narrative about the slapping incident. Doña Juana, it appears, had a secretary who fell in love with her and dared to write her a love letter. On receiving it, she gave no evidence of indignation, but the next day the secretary could be seen hanging in front of the palace windows. In his footnote, Tamayo explains that "the poet, unlike the chronicler, can well soften the Gothic cruelty of this account, adorning his work with more sweet and human sentiments. However, he will respect in his dramatic poem the symbol of the woman who was idolatrous of her honor." (*OC*, 565)

The impossible love of the enamored secretary appears in the first act, which is rather like a prologue.[24] The first scene, moreover, brings in the theme of Tristram and Iseult:

Act I, Scene i

(*Vivaldo, Doña Juana, Marina, and ladies. The first, seated at a desk, lays down a book he was reading from. The ladies are doing needlework on the opposite side of the stage.*)

VIVALDO. Poor Tristram!

MARINA. Didn't I say so? May he come to no good, King Mark! His wife, the beautiful Iseult, had reason to hate him, and turn her affection to the gallant, gentle youth.

VIVALDO. The king should have vanquished Tristram in the open field; but to kill him, sleeping. . . . Ay! Jealousy is base.

DOÑA JUANA. Say rather, that of foolish love the fruits are always bitter.

MARINA. Foolish love?

DOÑA JUANA. No more Tristram and Lancelot of the Lake. 'Tis a fiery pestilence of the soul, a poisonous book and vain.

VIVALDO. Take care, for it is truth and history.

DOÑA JUANA. You take care, I command it. Read again the noble deeds of our Castilian Cid or relate the history of my noble ancestors.

Tristram and Iseult represent courtly love, the foolish love (*amor loco*) of those who perish in their passion. There will be no such love in *Doña Juana the Magnate*, only, so to speak, Castilian love, which must end in marriage. Castilian love was one of the most cherished values of Manuel Tamayo y Baus.[25]

Doña Juana brings to mind the old national ballads of Spain, the *romances*. At the beginning of the play, the following ballad appears, in which Vivaldo tells Doña Juana of her husband's noble deed at the battle of Aljubarrota, where he lost his life:

> "If they have killed your horse, my king,
> you must rise up now on mine;
> and if pain steals your strength away,
> come, I'll lift you in my arms.

Raise your foot, in the stirrup place,
and the other upon my hands;
see how the crowd is pressing now,
though I die, you must go free.
My children lose their father,
but I save the father of all;
be the guardian of my family,
and Godspeed go in your van."
Thus spoke the brave Alavese,
lord of Hita and Buitrago,
to the King Don Juan the First
as he rushed to die in battle.[26]

This ballad may have come from one of three sources. It is first recorded in the *Romancero General* of 1600, but since Lope de Vega (1562-1635) and Luis Vélez de Guevara (1579-1644) inserted it in their plays, Tamayo may have taken it from them also. In any case, all of *Doña Juana the Magnate* contains the spirit of the ballads, which have been called "the real Iliad of Spain."

The traditional character of *Doña Juana* can also be seen in the many proverbs Tamayo put into it, especially in Act IV, Scene viii, where they are strung out the same way Sancho Panza used to utter them: "Not everything that whitens is flour"; "The cat that meows, a poor hunter I vow"; "For the dead ass, cats to the tail." There are, moreover, two brief stories in the play that resemble medieval exempla. Both are told by Doña Juana's vassal, Beltrán:

What an answer!
One day a rustic took
to the priest of his neighborhood
a certain little ass he had,
swearing that it could read
with singular achievement.
The priest, of torpid mind,
looked for and opened a tome:
the brainy ass regarded it;
but read? not by any sign.
He stayed there muter than mute.
Now the curate was annoyed,
and short of patience exclaimed:

"Does this animal read or no?"
On which the other replied:
"He is reading to himself." (*OC*, 526, 11-26)
. . . .

You are all alike. Women!
Who could ever understand you?
You do all and say all
always in reverse. How discreet
was our old neighbor
Ginés, the king's tax man.
On crossing the river one day
which is distant from here a league
with his wife and also his mare,
both of savage disposition,
behold the devil himself
came up with one of his schemes,
and into the river they fell,
the animal and the pair.
And then the patient man
caught a bush branch on the shore,
but saw that his poor rib
was a victim in the current.
Very convinced was Ginés
with no doubts about it at all
that women always and everywhere
do things backwards, in reverse;
so to help his wife, with anxious care
emerge from that travail
he did not go downstream
but went up-river to find her. (*OC*, 540, 39–541, 22)

At the ending of *Doña Juana the Magnate,* Tamayo departs
from the Pecha manuscript of 1635. According to Pecha, the
enamored secretary was hanged, but Tamayo, with his typical
happy ending, has him pardoned. And Doña Juana, the lady
magnate, concludes: "In virtue alone is there joy" (*OC*, 562, 23).
According to Tamayo's philosophy, life is a comedy. In the
unseen world, where St. Michael does battle with Lucifer, the
good forces eventually overcome the bad; and so in human life,
which has been redeemed at great price, virtue will one day
triumph in spite of the terrible odds. And there will be joy. This,
ultimately, is what Tamayo's theater is trying to tell us.[27]

IX   La locura de amor (The Madness of Love), *1855*

The evening of January 12, 1855, a crowd gathered at the doors of the Príncipe theater for the opening night of *The Madness of Love*. Everyone was anxious to see and hear the story of Doña Juana,[28] the mad queen of Castile, acted out on the stage, for word had spread that this was Tamayo's greatest play; the actors had praised it to their friends, the critics had constantly discussed it in the newspapers, the posters had announced it, and above all the *tertulias* (evening social gatherings) had made it their leading topic of discussion. The people crowded their way into every seat and impatiently waited for the curtain to go up. Finally, they heard the opening line:

ADMIRAL. I tell you, Don Juan Manuel, that vainly do you strive to convince me our queen Doña Juana is insane.

From the first scene, the audience became one with the action of the play and at the final curtain the applause was deafening. *The Madness of Love* was to be a favorite drama of the Spanish-speaking world.[29] And indeed, the story of Doña Juana la Loca (1479-1555), Queen of Castile, is one of the most dramatic episodes of Spanish history. The central years of this story are 1496-1506, the decade when Spain was becoming the most powerful nation in Europe.

Between 1474 and the end of the century, Juana's parents, Isabel and Ferdinand, the famous *Reyes Católicos* (Catholic Monarchs), had brought peace and order to Castile. The powers of the factious nobility were curbed, and with the cessation of civil war it appeared that the nation, under the guidance of able leaders, could accomplish great feats at home and broad. Columbus had discovered America, Nebrija had published his famous *Grammar,* Granada had been retaken, Cisneros, churchman, statesman, and regent of Castile, had proved an able counsellor, Gonzalo de Córdoba, the Great Captain, as he was named, had created a strong army—it seemed that Spain was to be the new Rome.

But this able leadership was threatened by a grave problem of succession. Although Ferdinand and Isabel had five children, Isabel, Juan, Juana, María, and Catalina, there were so many untimely deaths among them and their offspring, that by 1499 the third child, Juana, stood first in line to the throne. She was known to be mentally unstable, a trait hardly desirable in a political leader, and this was complicated by the fact that she had married a man who disdained Spain and all its customs. Her husband, Philip the Fair (1478-1506), was prepared to use Spanish political office to further the aims of himself and his Flemish followers.

As far as the succession was concerned, matters came to a head in November of 1504, on the death of Isabel the Catholic. Juana at the time was apparently unbalanced, for earlier in the year she had attacked a woman her husband was attentive to, and she had ordered her rival's hair cut off. Isabel's will specified that in case of her daughter's incapacity, her own husband, Ferdinand, should govern as regent until her young grandson, Charles, came of age. In spite of this provision, however, Juana and Philip ascended the throne. The next two years witnessed political jockeying between Juana's husband, Philip, and her father, Ferdinand. Juana sided with her father in this dispute, and an angry Philip had her confined. This act aggravated her illness.

In 1506 (the year Tamayo's play takes place), Philip was in fact ruling Spain, although Juana was the monarch before the law. He turned over all the political offices and favors to his own followers, who were not Spaniards. He became extremely unpopular, so much so that serious trouble was brewing, when he suddenly died, in the month of September.

Several historians have debated the insanity of Doña Juana. Was she really insane or did her apparently insane actions (her assault on a lady of the court, her refusal to eat or to change her clothes, her staying up one night, scantily clad, shivering in a courtyard, her refusal to give up her dead husband's body) have a cause other than true mental alienation? One biographer has argued that Juana was *loca de amor,* "crazy from love," but he was loudly answered by a later critic:

Writers as erudite as Mr. Rodríguez Villa have vainly tried to prove that Doña Juana was not really insane but extremely jealous, a woman in love; this thesis is only acceptable in the beautiful drama of Tamayo, *The Madness of Love,* since art is permitted this license and even greater ones.[30]

Perhaps one contemporary of Tamayo has posed the problem of Doña Juana's mental state better than anyone else. He made up a list of Juana's many curious actions, and then he asked himself: "Is this insanity?" To which he replied: "The historians say yes, and the poets say no."[31]

X   Tamayo's Drama

The Madness of Love begins on a historical note. It is 1506. Philip, Juana's consort, wants to have her put away, and some of the grandees, whose powers and wealth were curtailed by Juana's mother, the great Isabel, side with him. But he is opposed by other grandees and above all by the people. The people worship their Castilian monarchs, they detest the foreigner, Philip, and his Flemish followers.

The play soon turns from the historical events to the poetical theme, Love-Madness. Philip, in his own way, is mad, for in his numerous love affairs he is crazed by his desire for a woman. His "mad love" (*amor loco*) causes him to act irrationally and in the play he is culpable of as many outrageous actions as his spouse, Juana.

The Moorish girl, Aldara, is also crazed by love. In the entanglement (*enredo*) of the plot, her beauty deprives. Philip of his reason, and similarly she is deprived of her reason by her passion for the valorous captain, Don Alvar de Estúñiga. She will do anything to win his affection, even renounce her Moslem faith, but he does not requite her love. The mad actions of this woman match those of Doña Juana: she is, as Tamayo has it, "the panther of the desert" and Juana "the lioness of Castile." The scene in which these two women confront each other offers the most visible expression of madness in the play; Aldara provokes Juana to the mad point where she wants to duel with her, as if they were men; indeed, Juana's appearance, sword in hand, before the grandees of the realm, does more to discredit her in their eyes than anything else, for her action is truly irrational. Mad! Insane!

If there is a mad or wicked love, in which the passions overcome reason, there is also a rational love, a morally good or true love. This is the ordered love in which the faculties of the soul and body are directed to their proper ends. This love has a long tradition in Spanish literature; it is, for example, the love Cervantes saw in Marcela, Preciosa, Costanza, and even Camila, before her corruption by her foolish husband.

Rational love, to be sure, is one of the highest values of Tamayo's theater, and in his play it appears in the person of Don Alvar. This valorous captain loves his queen as a man does a woman, but his reason always controls his inclinations; his reason is, so to speak, *la cuerda de la casa* (the sane one in the house). Although he opposes King Philip, whose love-madness is responsible for so many crimes and also for the madness of his adored queen, he respects him for his position. Don Alvar, the sane man, has all the theological and cardinal virtues. These virtues are his values, and since they are also Tamayo's values, Don Alvar is really a portrait of Tamayo himself.

In one strange way, Doña Juana is the maddest of the crazed lovers, even though she keeps her love for her own husband. He is far more sinful than she, indeed he will not stop at murder, but she nevertheless has a terrible vice—jealousy. When she gives herself up to this monster she will do anything, even abandon a throne and the people, who need her. In brief, Philip is lascivious, Aldara and Juana jealous. Their love is not rational. Alvar, on the other hand, always controls his appetites with his reason and will.

The theme of love-madness carries in its train several variations. For the courtesans, for example, passionate love makes sense—it is the norm—whereas conjugal love stands outside the norm. "Outside the norm" is synonymous with "mad." But the courtesans are a corrupt lot, and here, as in many other plays, Tamayo introduces Antonio de Guevara's (1480-1545) idea of *menosprecio de corte y alabanza de aldea* (scorn of court and praise of village).

It was Cervantes who defined history as that which happened and poetry as that which might have happened or ought to have happened. Given these definitions, history and poetry seem to enjoy a singularly harmonious unity in the person of Doña Juana. When she says of her husband, "I will poison all his pleasures" (Act I, Sc. xi), the line rings true; the reader *knows* that the historical Juana did in fact say this, or that if she didn't say it, it is so characteristic of her, she might indeed have uttered those very words. When she orders the court ladies to gather and write their signatures so that she can identify the king's alleged lover, and when she pays more attention to their handwriting than to the grandees, who have gathered before her to discuss her fitness to rule, the reader will accept this as history, although on reflection he suspects it is probably poetic invention; it seems so true it might just as well have happened. This same verisimilitude is seen in many other scenes of the play, for example, Act II, Sc. i, where the carriers discuss the fate of their country. In short, Tamayo succeeds in conveying the historical sense of the years before 1506.

The great Isabel the Catholic is mentioned so often in the play that one can feel her presence in the Spain of that time. One senses the greed of the Flemish and Castilian followers of Philip, and also the disesteem in which the people held them. And finally, when the Admiral says that only the Cortes can judge Juana incapable of ruling and turn a regency over to Philip, one sees the spirit of the Spanish government before the advent of the Habsburgs.

The political theme of the play comes to a climax in Act IV, Sc. v, where Juana appears before all the nobles and prelates of the realm. In her absence, they have been discussing her demission as queen, when suddenly her voice is heard:

QUEEN. (*Doña Juana, with scepter, crown, and robe of state*). Make way for the Queen! (*Ascending the throne before the king.*)
KING. The Queen! (*Confused noises. General surprise.*)
MARQUIS. Doña Juana!
QUEEN. What unsettles and surprises you? Did you not count on my presence? Well, you reasoned badly. The doors of my rooms were closed; but they say there is a remedy for everything, if not death. They were ordered closed by the King, the Queen ordered them opened wide; Castilian loyalty outdid Flemish deceit, and here I am.
DON JUAN MANUEL. We must act quickly. (*In a low voice, to the king.*)
KING. Have the kindness to return to your abode, Madam.
QUEEN. There is no need. I know you were discussing grave affairs. You wish to enclose me in some strong fortress for the remainder of my life; you wish to make the crown that belongs to me alone the property of Don Philip of Austria.

This agreement is by all means necessary; I myself judge it to be so, and so I come to soften the pain that undoubtedly afflicts the tender heart of my husband; to repay the noble zeal that all of you have manifested in behalf of the common weal; and to say an eternal good-bye to the throne of my ancestors. And since I learned that you were annoyed at my poor black dress, to please you, and perhaps once more to appear to you to be the queen, I have put on, as you can see, my most splendid garments. (*She descends from the throne and addresses Don Juan Manuel and the other grandees with a delicate irony.*) May heaven keep you, Don Juan Manuel, lord of Belmonte de Campos, majordomo of my mother Doña Isabel, first Spanish Knight of the Golden Fleece of the house of Burgundy, and president of my Council. Your glory exceeds that of another Don Juan Manuel, whose learned pen made his name so famous, and whose intrepid steel subdued and destroyed the strong Ozmin, general of the House of Granada, on the shores of the Guadalquivir. Behold, gentlemen, a grandson of the Prince Don Juan Manuel, a descendant of the King St. Ferdinand and of the Emperors of Constantinople, converted today into an agent of the misconduct of an Archduke of Austria.

DON JUAN MANUEL. Madam!

Doña Juana goes on to humiliate other dignitaries of the court.

Tamayo was not content merely to write a play with the theme of love-madness; for him, this theme represents a moral problem that must be resolved. Consequently, in the final act (V), he writes the Happy Ending, which is characteristic of almost all his plays. According to Tamayo, life is a comedy, man has been redeemed (redemption is, so to speak, a form), and this truth must be represented on the stage, made palpable.

First, the audience learns that the tempestuous Moorish girl, Aldara, will be baptized and become a nun. Secondly, the king is dying and it seems certain that the queen will be put away. This means that the fatherland will soon suffer "a cruel orphanhood," but Don Alvar and other good Castilians will come to its aid.

King Philip dies at the end, but he dies well shriven. He has made his peace with God and man, and with his wife, Doña Juana, whom he loves now:

QUEEN. Do you love me?

KING. (*Rising*). With love I can't explain. Heaven wills for my punishment that my heart, which now will beat no longer, begins to adore you...... Juana! My Juana! What a horrible punishment! Eternal God, mercy!... Pardon! (*He dies.*)

Juana herself comes to a peaceful end, although she is clearly insane. It is said that in real life she clung morbidly to Philip's dead body, but in the play she is rather like a nurse keeping a nocturnal vigil:

QUEEN. Silence, my lords, silence!... The king has fallen asleep. Silence!... Do not wake him. Sleep, my love; sleep... sleep!...

The first four acts of *The Madness of Love* are an enjoyable experience in the theater. They are an imaginative, artistic blending of poetry and history, of Doña Juana as seen through Tamayo's eyes and of Doña Juana as the world knew her. The fifth act, however, is quite different. The audience of the 1850's delighted in its presentation of virtue triumphant and the Happy Ending, but another audience may look upon this as a contrivance or manipulation rather than an artistic creation. Be that as it may, Tamayo unquestionably had the knack of bringing tears to the eye.

CHAPTER 5

La bola de nieve (The Snowball)
and Un drama nuevo (A New Drama)

I *Tamayo: Verse or Prose*

A S we have observed above, during his first creative decade (1847-1856), Tamayo wrote half his plays in verse and the other half in prose. After that, in his second creative decade (1862-1870), he wrote everything in prose.

The Snowball was Tamayo's last attempt at verse, and one can see why he abandoned it. This play, together with *Joan of Arc, Virginia*, and *Doña Juana the Magnate*, shows that he was not completely at home in metrical writing. When he was using the combinations known as *romances* or *redondillas*,[1] he did rather well and the effect on the whole is agreeable. These meters are ordinarily used for narrative purposes; the *romances* are good for relating what has happened and for general exposition, the *redondillas* for a lively conversation.

Tamayo, however, seems incapable of writing other kinds of verse that characterize great works of art in the theater. One thinks of Segismundo's famous *décimas*[2] in Calderón's *Life Is a Dream*, Act I, Scene ii, where he compares his human state to that of the bird, beast, fish, and stream; or Act II, Scene xix, where he pronounces the famous lines "for all life is a dream, and dreams are dreams." These *décimas* are soliloquies, and on reflection one realizes that Tamayo does not write distinguished soliloquies—indeed, any soliloquy is rare in his work. He does not seem equal to the philosophical or plaintive note that a soliloquy requires.

Furthermore, Tamayo is not a lyrical playwright. Take, for example, Lope de Vega's *Caballero de Olmedo*, in which the cavalier, Don Alonso, leaves his lady, Inés, and recites the amorous, conceptist lines:

74

I leave, and leave to my death,
although dying I do not leave you,
for if the soul will not go,
how is it possible I leave you
or how much more return to see you?

These verses of Don Alonso are known as *quintillas*,[3] which
are generally employed to express deep emotions of a pathetic
and lyrical character.[4] It is doubtful that Tamayo could ever
write verses such as these; the fact is, he did not.

In plays written in verse, moreover, one might occasionally
expect a sonnet, with its singular unity and brilliant idea. A
good example is the demon's sonnet in Mira de Amescua's *Slave
of the Devil*, where he describes his vengeance (Act III, vv.
2692-2705); or the sonnets of García and Blanca in Rojas Zorrilla's *No One Beneath the King*, where they profess their great
love (Act I, vv. 291-318); or of Diana in Agustín Moreto's *Treat
Disdain with Disdain*, when she speaks of the fire in her heart
(Act III, vv. 2553-66).[5] Tamayo writes no sonnets such as these.

Tamayo apparently had no lyre to pluck while he sang. He had
a story to relate, a message to convey, an action to get on with,
and for these tasks he found prose a vehicle better adapted to
his capacities than verse.

There is also a historical reason for Tamayo's changing to
prose as he passed from his first to his second creative decade.
Fernán Caballero had written the first of her novels with local
color as early as 1849, and Benito Pérez Galdós was to write the
first of his fourscore novels in 1868. Tamayo, then, writing *The
Snowball* in 1856, stood at the threshold of a new era. Through
a kind of literary inertia, he still wrote in verse in 1856, but
starting with the plays of 1862 and 1863 he would write only in
prose. In this sense, he represents the advent of realism to the
Spanish stage, for people in thesis plays and plays about high
society must speak as they speak in real life, that is, in prose.

II   The Snowball: *The Meaning and the Form*

The Snowball tells the story of a brother and sister, Luis and
Clara, who are extremely jealous persons. Luis is betrothed to
an orphan girl, María, and Clara to a young gentleman, Fer-

nando. Luis' imagination makes him think María is interested in someone else, and Clara's imagination makes her think Fernando has his heart elsewhere; the unfounded suspicions of the jealous pair grow and grow (they snowball—hence the title) and their behavior worsens progressively until they alienate their fiancés, who will marry each other.

In the first act, Tamayo succeeds in uniting the form of the play with the meaning. Clara and Luis talk in such a way (Act I, Scene xii) that the audience senses a crescendo; he is talking, she is talking; he is jealous, she is jealous; he ignites her fears, she his; he speaks more quickly, she more quickly; he repeats her words, she repeats his; and so forth. Thus the pace quickens and there is a snowballing in the structure of the language as well as in the meaning, where the jealous brother and sister destroy their own happiness. Tamayo uses this same style in other parts of the play, e.g., Act II, Scene xii.

In Act III, Clara, the jealous woman, says to María, the orphan: "I have changed a lot." She is contrite because her brother Luis wants to duel with Fernando and kill him. Act III presents the Tamayesque Happy Ending, the most unusual perhaps of his happy endings.[6] There is terrible violence and contumely, and the language leaves the reader uncomfortable (how much more uncomfortable would an audience be!), but the jealous Clara and Luis finally ask God to make their former fiancés, Fernando and María, happy (¡Hazla dichosa, Dios mío! ... ¡Dios eterno, hazle dichoso!). This spiritual conversion is unseemly, given the prior violence and contumely.[7]

Every one of the three acts begins with a scene in which the servants, Juana and Pedro, chatter away and advance the action of the following scenes. Juana and Pedro represent Tamayo's attempt to introduce the gracioso (the figure of fun) into his theater, and as such they are more like Calderón's gracioso than Lope's: they are a vile pair.[8]

In the fourth scene, Act I, the reader learns that María was an orphan:

MARIA.   When two years ago heaven
          with its invincible power
          deprived me of that mother
          who was my only support.

From this point on the figure of the Orphan is one of the principal images in the play. Apparently the nineteenth century delighted in characters that one might call extreme, such as the miser and the orphan,[9] and Tamayo was giving the audience what it was seeking. An orphan! A girl without a mother! The ultimate in abandonment! And at the end she can find a protector in the young gentleman, Fernando, whose care for the poor girl constitutes a kind of redemption. *The Snowball* throws light on Tamayo's doctrine of forms, which he considered to be the proper object of the theater.[10]

Tamayo and his nineteenth-century audiences delighted in categories that might be called Forms, Ideas, Archetypes, or Ultimates. These could be put on the stage where, in the dress of human beings, they could be enjoyed by the spectators. There are the general categories of Evil and Good, and specific Forms or Ideas fall within them. Thus there are:

	Evil	*Good*
The Snowball	Orphanhood	Redemption
The Snowball	Jealousy	Trust
Daughter and Mother[11]	Ingratitude	Filial Love
Madness of Love	Foolish Love	Good Love
Madness of Love	Greed	Selflessness in God
Virginia	Lust	Chastity
Duels of Honor	Pride	Humility
Duels of Honor	Murder	Charity
The Upright Men	Scandal	Righteous Anger
The Right Track	Greed	Charity
The Right Track	Egoism	Humility
Actions Speak Louder	Hypocrisy	Truthfulness
Actions Speak Louder	Selfishness	Charity

In the 1850's and 1860's, Tamayo owed his outstanding success in the theater to his ability to present these forms and categories better than any other playwright. To most twentieth-century critics, who do not accept these forms and categories, his plays seem stilted and banal.[12]

III   Un drama nuevo (A New Drama), 1867

The uniqueness of *A New Drama* takes the reader of Tamayo by surprise. There is nothing else quite like it in the corpus of his work. The earlier plays are written in the manner of Schiller or Lope, or they are based on a passage of Livy that was the source of other dramas. The later plays are contentious or given to preaching a moral; moreover, the shaping of their plot reveals too much external contrivance on the part of the author and a lack of internal growth on the part of the characters. This leads to the rhetoric of the *raisonneur,* who is wont to spell things out for the audience. The author apparently looked upon the audience as a big child.

But *A New Drama* was somehow different. Of Tamayo's plays, it has always been the critics' favorite. Writing in the nineteenth century, Padre Blanco García called it "the most admirable and the most admired of his works,"[13] and more recently Professor Angel del Río, who was only mildly impressed by Tamayo's other plays, has stated:

The introduction to the stage in 1867 of an original topic that was complex in its artistic meaning, such as *A New Drama,* showed a boldness and a sense of theater much superior to that of the age.[14]

Finally, one might consider the college classroom of the decade in which the present book was composed, the 1970's. The professor who teaches a nineteenth-century drama course may come upon his students a year or two after they leave him. On mentioning the class to them, he will find that they remember above all Tamayo's *A New Drama.*

Tamayo had always admired Shakespeare, and he decided to write a play with him as one of the main characters. In *A New Drama,* Shakespeare is the director of a theater company who is always on the lookout for new plays to stage. A young author comes and gives him a manuscript, *A New Drama.* Shakespeare likes it and will produce it. The play has four characters. Its theme is jealousy. Count Octavio is a middle-aged man who has an adopted son, Manfredo, and a young wife, Beatriz, who fall in love with each other and rob Octavio of his honor. He learns about the nefarious love from a letter his enemy, Landolfo, gives to him. In a rage, he duels with Manfredo.

In casting the play, Shakespeare decides to give the main role, the tragic figure of Octavio, to a comic actor called Yorick.[15]

This infuriates a man named Walton, who feels slighted since he is the company's leading tragic actor. He must settle for the part of Landolfo. The other two actors in the drama are Alicia, Yorick's young wife, and Edmundo, his adopted son. They will play Beatriz and Manfredo.

Now the reader finds Tamayo creating a play-within-a-play, with singular unity. In real life (the real life of *A New Drama*) the circumstances of the actors are the same as those of the characters they must portray. Yorick's wife, Alicia, is in truth in love with Edmundo, his son, and he with her.[16] Walton really hates Yorick and envies him, and in the course of the action he takes a stage-prop letter and replaces it with an authentic letter showing that Yorick's wife and son are unfaithful to him. As the tragedy of Count Octavio reaches its climax, Yorick is so blinded with rage he gets carried away and becomes Octavio. When he duels with his son Edmundo (cast as Manfredo) on the stage, he stabs him to death.[17] The play can no longer go on. The Author, the Prompter, the stagehands, and all the actors and employees of the theater come forth to view the dead man's body. These persons blend into one the imaginary audience of Count Octavio, Beatriz, Manfredo, and Landolfo, and the real audience of Tamayo.

Outside of Yorick, the most prominent character in the play is William Shakespeare. It is he who fuses the history of flesh-and-blood men (Tamayo and his audience) and the history, or story, of fictitious men (the young author with the manuscript and his characters). Yorick fears and loves Shakespeare, Walton fears and admires him, Edmundo and Alicia seek his help, and the young author and the Prompter treat him with deference.[18]

Tamayo's Shakespeare is rather like the author of the autobiographical novel, which is written in the first person. He is intimate. He is close to things. He makes them believable. At the same time, he also resembles the author of a realistic novel written in the third person. He is omniscient. He has a perfect command of his universe. In *A New Drama*, Shakespeare is here and there and everywhere. He is both a member of the fictitious world and a godlike being that is creating it.[19]

IV *Act I*

The first act opens with a scene in Yorick's house, where he
and Shakespeare are talking. The presence of Shakespeare over-
whelms the other figures of the play and, one suspects, Tamayo
himself, for Shakespeare has an unusual strength of character. In
the first scene, he sees through Yorick's flattery but nevertheless
grants him the coveted role. Yorick then has a long scene to
himself in which he opens the manuscript of *A New Drama* and
reads the same lines he will recite at the end of Act III:

> May she tremble, the faithless wife, let the ingrate tremble
> who purloins my honor and my joy.
> Your precaution was in vain
> And here you see the token of your sin.
> (*He opens the letter.*)
> My blood runs cold.
> (*Without daring to look at the letter.*)
> May it warm again in wrath!
> Woe to the villain for whom you debase me, blinded!
> Oh! What do I see? Dear Christ! Oh Christ a thousand times!

He reads further into the manuscript and encounters the line
¿Conque eres tú el villano . . .? ("And so you are the villain?"),
which he rehearses four times. He comments on how he ought
to read it. This will be the dramatic line that he utters in the
third act when he realizes that the unknown lover is his own
son, Edmundo.

Yorick now speaks with Edmundo, whom he chides for being
reserved. "Why do you stay away from me?" he asks. Their lines
are subtly ambiguous and gradually Tamayo weaves the net of
dramatic intrigue about them. Yorick speaks to Edmundo and
then recites a line from the new manuscript: "May she tremble,
the faithless wife . . . !" A few lines later he will say to Edmundo,
who is alarmed: "You are pale now. . . . Your hand trembles"
(*Tu mano tiembla*). Yorick fails to note the resemblance between the theatrical trembling (*tiemble*) of "the faithless wife"
and the trembling (*tiembla*) of Edmundo in real life, but it
does not escape the ear of the audience. Tamayo carefully
grounds his play on musical mnemonics.

Walton now appears, with Yorick and Edmundo still on the

stage, and he intentionally continues the double meaning that
Yorick had originated, unintentionally, in an earlier scene. This
tortured soul feigns no joy at Yorick's selection for the role of
Octavio. When Yorick asks him to help him with his lines, he
works his venom into his reply:

YORICK. Well then, let's go to my room, there we can shut ourselves
in. Frankly the role of an outraged husband seems on the
difficult side to me.
WALTON. You are deceived. It is quite easy to play the outraged
husband. I wager Edmundo is of the same opinion.
EDMUNDO. Me? (What can this man be saying?)

In the next scene, where Edmundo and Alicia are alone and
speak of their love, Tamayo displays the same weakness that
appears in his other plays: it is difficult for him to create a
natural or smoothly flowing conversation between a man and
a woman. Edmundo and Alicia are two lovers caught in a passion
bordering on incest, a dark passion that brings to mind the
Greek tragedies, an inferno, or a paradise lost, and so they might
use extraordinary words not usually given to lovers, words evoking social doom or metaphysical chaos; but the structure of
Tamayo's language is not equal to the task. Here are a few
examples from Act I, Scene v, in Spanish and English:

EDMUNDO. *¡Siempre recelar! ¡Siempre temer! ¡Ay qué asustadiza es
la culpa! ¡Ay qué existencia la del culpado!*
(Always suspicious! Always afraid! Oh how readily alarmed
is sin! Oh what an existence that of the sinner!)
. . . .
EDMUNDO. *Serénate, Alicia, y considera que, a serlo más, te creería
menos culpada. Parece siempre horrenda la culpa si aun brilla
a su lado la virtud.*
(Be calm, Alicia, and remember that I, being more guilty,
consider you less to blame. Sin always seems horrendous if
virtue still shines at its side.)
. . . .
ALICIA. *No me hables de virtud. Sólo con amarte huello todos los
deberes; ofendo al cielo y a la tierra. Sálvame; salva, como
fuerte, a una débil mujer.*
(Don't speak to me of virtue. Just by loving you, I trample

upon all duty; I offend heaven and earth. Save me; as a
strong man, save a weak woman.)
. . . .

EDMUNDO. *¡Oh, sí; preciso es que ambos nos salvemos! Pero ¿cómo
salvarnos?*
(Oh yes; we must both save ourselves! But how?)

These lines make the reader wonder if Tamayo's limitation is
not so much literary as theological, a kind of Jansenism that
binds his theater to a code rather than to the experience of human
life (or to the forms he professed to see in nature).[20] At this
point in the play, Edmundo and Alicia have not committed
adultery, except perhaps in their own mind. They have not
united their flesh, although they have thought constantly of
each other in their infatuation. Apparently they think that such
a strong attraction is in itself evil, that the very thought of
such a thing is sinful ("Oh how readily alarmed is sin! Oh
what an existence that of the sinner!"), and that an intention,
however unexpressed in action it may be, is as bad as the act
itself. And the intentions they consider bad are indeed hesi-
tant, for they are constantly struggling with them throughout
the play. In Act I, Scene v, Edmundo and Alicia "start to embrace and stop, upon hearing a noise in the background"; this
suggests that they may have embraced before, but this is the
extent of their crime. In Act III they plan to run away, and
Edmundo indeed contracts with a sea captain to take them
aboard, but Alicia repents before they go and her words lead
us to believe she would not have run off with Edmundo had he
lived. In other words, Edmundo and Alicia are living in a kind
of halfway house, between natural desires that are beautiful in
themselves and terrible crimes that recall Lucifer rebelling
against the Almighty. They are, one suspects, two innocent young
people who have a terrible fire in their breasts to contend with,
but Tamayo ascribes to them a sin they are not guilty of. It
follows that the language he creates to reveal their plight will
not be the language of a man like Shakespeare. Macbeth really
did plunge his dagger into a man. He may also imagine that
he plunged it, but he imagines this because he actually had
performed the deed.

The words of Edmundo: "Oh yes; we must both save ourselves! But how?" again, have a Jansenistic air. A Christian may ultimately have the thought of salvation stamped in him, but it is not the first thought to come into his mind in a given crisis. It is not proximate. A nearly incestuous pair, a man who is figuratively killing his father and marrying his mother, will talk of sorrow and despair, of fear and punishment, of the innocent and guilty, of the good and the damned, of love and the passions, of the mountain heights and depths of the sea, of metaphysical order and chaos, and perhaps finally of doom (the Greeks) or hope and salvation (the Golden Age Spanish), but they will not ask, "How can we save ourselves?" Persons who ask such a question may lead a miserable life, but they are not doomed, or saved by an ineffable grace; they are not the stuff a Shakespearean or Calderonian play is made of.[21]

In the last scene of Act I, Shakespeare has a long talk with Alicia and Edmundo, in which he declares he is aware of their love. He promises to help them. There is one obstacle, the envious Walton, but Shakespeare feels he can use his authority to keep him in line; Walton stands in awe of the great poet.

The dramatic ending of Act I is one of the most memorable scenes in Tamayo's theater. Shakespeare, Edmundo, and Alicia have had a long talk and the action has been at a standstill. Yorick, accompanied by Walton, walks out on the stage and rehearses his lines. He has not yet dominated the role of Octavio, and he is overacting:

YORICK. (*Seizing his wife by an arm in an overtragic manner and pronouncing his words with too much emphasis.*) May she tremble, the faithless wife, let the ingrate tremble . . .
ALICIA. Dear God! (*Shuddering with fright.*) Pardon! (*Falling to the ground unconscious.*)
YORICK. Eh?
EDMUNDO. (*Wanting to throw himself on Walton.*) Scoundrel!
SHAKESPEARE. (*In a low voice to Edmundo, detaining him.*) Fool!
WALTON. (*Ironically.*) What a coincidence!
YORICK. Pardon! (*Trying to explain to himself what has happened. Shakespeare goes to help Alicia.*)

The curtain descends. The ingenuous Yorick now knows.

V *Acts II and III*

After he has finished Acts II and III, it dawns on the reader why *A New Drama* is such a popular play. In dramatizing the story of Yorick, Edmundo, Alicia, and Walton, Tamayo has followed the formula laid down, or observed, by Lope de Vega in 1609 in his *New Art of Writing Plays*.[22] In this disquisition (in verse), Lope says he writes his plays the way people want them. He is aware of the precepts and unities established by antiquity, but he does not obey them, for if he did so he would lose his public. He is not legislating new precepts; he is merely describing the things he sees and practices in the theater, and he knows from experience that they work. The audiences love them.

Lope says that a play should have three acts, not four, and then he adds:

> In the first act present the problem (*caso*),
> in the second tie up the events
> so that until the middle of the third act
> nobody can judge how it will end.

This is precisely what Tamayo does in *A New Drama,* where in the second part of Act III the actors stage the play-within-the-play, the drama of Count Octavio, Manfredo, Beatriz, and Landolfo. The outcome is covered with uncertainty until Yorick (Octavio) stabs Edmundo (Manfredo). Lope's audiences loved such a performance, and so did Tamayo's, two hundred and fifty years later. Lope again:

> But do not permit the solution to take place
> until the arrival of the final scene
> because the crowd on knowing how it ends
> will turn its face to the door and its back
> on what it waited for three hours face to face;
> for there is nothing more to know than the way it ends.

According to Lope:

> The cases of honor are the best,
> because they powerfully move all people,
> and with them virtuous actions,
> for virtue is everywhere loved.

These lines were so true in Lope's day that after a play people would shun the villain and not sell him things he wished to buy, whereas they would wine and dine the hero; even dignitaries would do so.

Apparently the same rules applied in Tamayo's day. *A New Drama* is a "case of honor," in which Yorick is troubled by the faithlessness of his wife, and Shakespeare is the virtuous man whom everyone loves. According to one source, *A New Drama* was a publishing success as well as a stage success in its first year. It went through four printings.[23]

In other verses Lope states that equivocation and ambiguity are desirable:

> Equivocal speech and ambiguous
> incertitude have always had
> a great place in the crowd's heart
> because it thinks it alone understands what the other is saying.

Tamayo has followed this advice of Lope more closely than any other. There is a "persistent play of ambiguities" in Yorick's drama.[24]

Lope calls for repetition: anadiplosis, the special kind of repetition by which one begins a clause with a word from the previous clause, and anaphora. The reader has already seen examples of Tamayo's repetition in *A New Drama*; for examples of anadiplosis and anaphora, he might examine Act I, Scene vi, where Edmundo and Alicia speak to each other in brief, rapid sentences, in the presence of Shakespeare.

According to Lope, the crowd loves to see a woman disguised as a man. Although there is no such disguise in *A New Drama*, there is something similar in the disguise of the play-within-the-play, where the characters appear with names and costumes other than their own. The male disguise (*disfraz varonil*), in any case, is part of Lope's insistence on ambiguity, which Tamayo clearly followed.

Lope calls for one thing that Tamayo was clearly a master of:

> Let it rarely happen that the stage
> be without a person who speaks,
> for in those gaps the crowd becomes uneasy
> and the story drags out a great while.

Nearly every critic of Tamayo has alluded to his ability to move people on and off the stage. He does so without a feeling of abruptness, in *A New Drama* as well as his other plays.

Lope has one dictum that Tamayo makes peculiar use of in his play:

> With prudence make the verses conform
> to the subjects that are being treated.
> The *décimas* are good for plaints,
> the sonnet good for those who await another,
> the *romances* for narration
> although this comes out brilliant too in *octavas*.

Tamayo wrote nearly all of *A New Drama* in prose, so that the observation of Lope, "let the verses conform to the subjects," does not strictly apply to all his words. Nevertheless, in one sense Tamayo followed Lope's rule; all of *A New Drama* is written in prose except the second part of Act III, which appears in verse. The parent play of Tamayo, then, is written in prose, and the play of the fictitious young author, the theater-within-the-theater, is written in verse, especially *silvas*, which permits the affronted Count Octavio (Yorick) to express his strong emotions. Thus Tamayo makes a peculiarly good adaptation of Lope's advice: "let the verses conform to the subjects."

Lope tells why his abandonment of ancient rules makes for delightful theater:

> I maintain, in short, what I have written [his plays]
> and I know that even if they were better,
> in another mode they would not contain the pleasure that they do,
> because at times what opposes correctness
> for that very reason delights the fancy.

Lope is here arguing on a medieval principle, *contra factum non valet illatio* (an argument against the facts is not a valid argument). We may apply this principle to Tamayo. *A New Drama* has a lively plot, honor, equivocation, ambiguity, repetition, disguise, dexterous stage entrances, suitable verses, suspense, and a carefully concealed solution. No matter what objections one may bring against it, no matter how it "opposes correctness," its variety delights the audience, and according to Lope that is what theater is for:

for this variety delights a great deal.
A good example we are given by nature
who because of her variety is beautiful.[25]

VI *The Title*

Tamayo's title, *A New Drama*, brings to mind *The New Comedy* (1792) of Moratín, the author who represented French neoclassicism in Spain; Moratín, moreover, translated the works of Molière and looked to him as a model. Thus Tamayo seems to be saying that his title is ambiguous or even ironic, that within the fiction of his play there is a new drama (a new manuscript) written by a new young author, a contemporary of Shakespeare, but his play itself is not a new drama, it is as old as Shakespeare and the Elizabethan revenge dramas, it is as old as life itself, it is the story of human jealousy, which appears in the persons of Walton and Yorick.

CHAPTER 6

Some Early Plays

A list of Tamayo's dramatic works may vary from thirty-five to fifty entries, depending on how many of his rearrangements of foreign plays are included.[1] Some of these rearrangements are much further removed from the original plays than others; for example, *No hay mal que por bien no venga* (*Every Evil Hath Its Good*) is not so much a copy of Théodore Barrière's *Le Feu au Couvent* as an original work of Tamayo; whereas *Tran-Tran*, which he wrote in collaboration with his brother Victorino, is much closer to the original French of Bayard y Biéville's *Les Enfants de Troupe*.

The 1947 Fax edition of Tamayo's *Obras completas* (*Complete Works*) contains seventeen plays and the speech he gave on his entrance into the Royal Academy. The reader should note that so-called *Complete Works* in Spanish are often not complete; they may contain almost all of the author's works, or, as in the Fax edition of Tamayo, those considered truly his and of these only the best.

Here is the Fax list: *Juana de Arco* (*Joan of Arc*), 1847, *Una apuesta* (*A Wager*), 1851, *La esperanza de la patria* (*Her Country's Hope*), 1851, *Ángela* (*Ángela*), 1852, *Huyendo del perejil* (*Out of the Frying Pan*), 1853, *Virginia* (*Virginia*), 1853,[2] *La ricahembra* (*Doña Juana the Magnate*), 1854, *La locura de amor* (*The Madness of Love*), 1855, *Hija y madre* (*Daughter and Mother*), 1855, *La bola de nieve* (*The Snowball*), 1856, *Lo positivo* (*The Right Track*), 1859, *Lances de honor* (*Duels of Honor*), 1863, *Del dicho al hecho* (*Actions Speak Louder*), 1863, *Más vale maña que fuerza* (*Cunning Rather Than Force*), 1866, *Un drama nuevo* (*A New Drama*), 1867, *No hay mal que por bien no venga* (*Every Evil Hath Its Good*), 1868, and *Los hombres de bien* (*The Upright Men*), 1870. The present book has discussed all of these plays except *La esperanza de la patria*

88

and *Hija y madre*. It will now take up these two, and also five of Tamayo's early works, which may be found in *The Oberlin College Spanish Drama Collection*. The "Oberlin five" are the following: *El cinco de agosto* (*The Fifth of August*), 1849, *Tran-Tran* (*Tran-Tran*), 1850, *Una aventura de Richelieu* (*An Adventure of Richelieu*), 1851, *El castillo de Balsaín* (*The Castle of Balsaín*), 1851, and *Don Simplicio Bobadilla* (*Don Simplicio Bobadilla*), 1853.

I La esperanza de la patria (Her Country's Hope)

A *loa*, for Tamayo, is a short dramatic poem paying tribute to a famous person or famous event.[3] It is usually allegorical. *Her Country's Hope* is a *loa* which Tamayo wrote in collaboration with Manuel Cañete to celebrate the birth of Queen Isabel's first child, the Princess of Asturias.

The Chorus sounds a note of tribulation and the first of the allegorical figures, Spain, says that she has suffered a long time and finally rid herself of French domination and civil war.[4] But how much longer must she suffer? The Chorus sings the praises of God and Religion, which are the hope of Spain. Then the Virtues—Justice, Wisdom, and Valor—come to say they will inspire the newborn child. They meet the opposition of Anarchy and Despotism, but in turn these are opposed by Religion and Liberty. In the last scene, a crib appears with the new princess, and the queen her mother, Doña Berenguela and Isabel the Catholic at her side. Liberty and Religion declare: "We are always sisters!"

Although Tamayo will not be remembered for this *loa*, whose heptasyllables, octosyllables, decasyllables, hendecasyllables, and alexandrines are undistinguished,[5] it shows his ability to create a dramatic conflict even when writing a eulogy for an official occasion. It also provides a key to his vision of the Spanish State, which was decidedly *ancien régime*.[6]

II Hija y Madre (Daughter and Mother), *1855*

Daughter and Mother, in three acts, tells the story of a countess who is to marry a wealthy duke for his money. She herself is loved by a gentleman, Don Luis. Sixteen years before the action of the play, the countess had fallen in love and run away from her father. Later on she had a daughter, but fate punished her when a bandit came and kidnapped the young child. In the play, the countess is preparing for a great social occasion when two beggars, an old man and a young girl, come seeking alms. The countess recognizes the old man as her father and she turns him away, fearing that his disreputable state will endanger her wedding plans with the duke. Neither she nor anyone else realizes that the girl accompanying the old man is her daughter.

After a great deal of sobbing and pleading on the part of the principal characters, the play concludes with the expected Tamayesque Happy Ending. The countess gives up social appearances and the duke's gold for the sake of her father, and her virtue is rewarded when she learns that the young girl is her long-lost daughter. Don Luis, the man who loves the countess, marvels at this goodness and one suspects that the countess will marry him.

Daughter and Mother is worthy of attention because it represents a transition in Tamayo. Before its appearance in 1855, he had written plays whose primary goal was theatrical enjoyment (*deleite*), plays such as *Joan of Arc, A Wager, Ángela, Out of The Frying Pan, Virginia, Madness of Love,* and *Doña Juana the Magnate.* After 1855, he turned to plays with a moral. *Daughter and Mother,* with its bizarre tale, does not belong exactly to the *alta comedia,* but its tearful rhetoric, sudden conversions, and general lack of verisimilitude announce a new era in Tamayo's theater.

In *Daughter and Mother,* Tamayo does something that every Spanish author does at one time in his life or another: he pays tribute to the greatest of all Spanish writers, Cervantes. The play imitates, perhaps unconsciously, the exemplary novels, especially *La gitanilla* (*The Little Gypsy*) and *La ilustre fregona* (*The Illustrious Kitchen Maid*). First of all, old Andrew, the father of the countess, was brought up amongst the gypsies:

I never knew my parents, and in a Galician town gypsies brought me up, from whom I fled as soon as I could. The wife I later knew died, leaving me a father. Do you hear? I was a father! Father of a little girl so pretty that the people stopped enraptured in the middle of the street on seeing her pass by. Heaven blessed my efforts, and I succeeded in raising her to be a young lady. She was just sixteen years old and one day. . . . What a day! I looked for her everywhere; I waited for her, in vain. . . . Oh, woe is me! She had fled, sir; she had abandoned her father.

This whole passage, with the exception of the lachrymose abandonment, has a certain ring of Cervantes to it. Tamayo's "enraptured" (*embelesada*) may not have the same dignity as Cervantes' "amazed" (*suspenso, atónito, pasmado, admirado*), but it is unquestionably a nineteenth-century cousin.

Secondly, Tamayo's entire play points to the anagnorisis at the end. Some of the characters know that the countess is really old Andrew's daughter and that she deserted him when she was sixteen, but no one knows that the little girl, María, who accompanies Andrew as a sort of *lazarillo* (guide), is the countess' daughter, not even Andrew himself. She was kidnapped by the bandit José Ruiz many years before, and he now, like the gypsy woman in Cervantes' exemplary novel, reveals his secret. The reunion of María with the countess and the thrill it is supposed to create is similar to the reunion of Preciosa with the Comendador and his wife in *La gitanilla.*

Finally, Tamayo's eulogy of parental and filial ties is an attempt at exemplarity in the manner of Cervantes. In his search for exemplarity, Tamayo never achieves the artistic illumination that Cervantes does in his peerless novels, but however humble it may be, the same quest is there. Tamayo, a competent playwright of the nineteenth century, has honored the greatest author of the Golden Age.

Daughter and Mother is one vast *deus ex machina.* The bandit José Ruiz says as much in Act I, Scene v: "You see how, when God wills it, things/ wind up right in your hand." There is also such an emphasis on the unity of time in the play that an extraordinary number of things happen in one evening and a day. The effect is not unpleasant, and the audience of 1855 must have delighted in the rapid action and spectacle.

Lastly, it should be noted that the twenty-six-year-old Tamayo dedicates his play to Cándido Nocedal (1821-1885), the famous Carlist. In this dedication he writes some revealing words:

Our friendship was born yesterday, today it seems an old one; and just as you delight in seeing my efforts as a dramatic author rewarded, so I delight in seeing you defend . . . your innermost convictions in the difficult field of politics.

As a young man Tamayo already had strong ties with the Carlists.

III   El cinco de agosto (The Fifth of August)
El castillo de Balsaín (The Castle of Balsaín)

In 1849, the young Tamayo wrote *The Fifth of August* and in 1851, *The Castle of Balsaín*. These two plays might be called melodramas with a Christian message, in the Romantic style, or perhaps even Romantic plays *a lo divino*.[7]

The Fifth of August is set in the eleventh century, near a ruined castle, and the scenes take place at night. There is a red-headed hunchedback count, a mysterious ubiquitous Pilgrim, a father who poisons a lad that turns out to be his son, a poisoned youth rising from his tomb, and an instantaneous conversion. The evil count becomes good, true love wins out (in a way), the lady Alberta recognizes her long vanished husband in the Pilgrim, and count and son and Pilgrim go off to the Holy Land on a Crusade.

In *The Castle of Balsaín*, Justino, of common birth, loves a countess on whom the king has cast his lustful eye. The countess loves Justino, but cannot return his love since she is of noble birth; until, at the end, in the ruins of a castle, by the light of the moon, she learns that Justino is the king's unknown bastard son.[8] The king accepts his son and declares that he wants him to marry the countess.

The reader is struck by the Romantic setting of these plays and by Tamayo's imitating such works as Larra's *El doncel de don Enrique el doliente* (1834), Espronceda's *Sancho Saldaña* (1834), or Gil y Carrasco's *El señor de Bembibre* (1844). In their language and their use of a word such as *fate* (*sino*), the plays also resemble Goethe's *Sorrows of Young Werther* and the Duke of Rivas' *Don Alvaro, or The Force of Fate*. Here are a few examples of the Romantic trappings:

At last we are alone!
You have mocked me this day!
To the carnivorous wolf you have delivered
The timid lamb!
The one star of my gloomy night
You have extinguished.
I will drink your blood.
>   (*Fifth of August,* Act I, Sc. xii)

A volcano I have in my mind,.
In my breast another volcano.
>   (*Fifth of August,* Act II, Sc. vii)

An eternity entire,
I waited for him.
I have suffered.
>   (*Fifth of August,* Act II, Sc. ii)

She casts a diabolical glance.
>   (stage directions, *Fifth of August,* Act II, Sc. ii)

Today, my love, I try
the rigor of my fate.
>   (*Fifth of August,* Act II, Sc. iv)

Enough, oh enemy fate!
How long must I be your plaything!
>   (*Fifth of August,* Act II, Sc. vii)

without hope in heaven's mercy.
>   (*Fifth of August,* Act IV, Sc. iv)

Some angel has brought you here.
>   (*Balsaín,* Act I, Sc. ii)

I am the most unfortunate lover on earth.
>   (*Balsaín,* Act I, Sc. ii)

Then I fled my native town:
the solitary ruins
where you were born served as my abode,
and as food the game of these savage
forests.   (*Balsaín,* Act I, Sc. iii)

In spite of scores of passages such as these, neither of these plays has a true Romantic ring to it; neither gives evidence of the metaphysical crisis characteristic of the Romantic period.[9] Tamayo's intellect in no way doubts the truths of revealed religion, nor is his intellect in conflict with his will (his heart or his passions). For Tamayo, the intellect is able to receive biblical truth and the will, by its very nature, will embrace it. There is no somber cosmos, no outrage, no sense of being caught or tricked, no real sense of fate (*sino*), no rupture with tradition. Tamayo's plays are only superficially Romantic;[10] his religious convictions are as firm as those of a twelfth-century Crusader, who says in his play:

> I shall join the troop
> that will plant the holy tree
> of the Cross divine
> before Salem at the wall,
> which already crumbles beneath its vivid light.
> I shall rescue the tomb
> the fiery Muslim steals
> from the pale of Christian love.
> *(Fifth of August*, Act IV, Last Scene)

IV   Tran-Tran, *1850*

Tran-Tran, written by Tamayo and his brother Victorino, is a musical farce that stays very close to the original French.[11] Clara, the colonel's daughter, is to marry a foolish captain who is trying on a corset at the dressmaker's shop. Tran-Tran, the regimental drummer boy, knows about the corset and vows to help the young lieutenant, Luis, who loves and is loved by Clara. Tran-Tran is so successful with his antics that Luis and Clara will indeed get married, and finally Tran-Tran learns he is Clara's brother.

Plays such as *Tran-Tran*, rearranged from the French, did well at the box office and occupied a good part of Tamayo's attention.

V   Una aventura de Richelieu
(An Adventure of Richelieu), *1851*

An Adventure of Richelieu, another arrangement from the French, tells the story of the lascivious Duc de Richelieu, a Don

Juan who loves scandal more than women. He poses as his own secretary, he has a house with a secret door, he bribes a coachman to bring a married woman there, and he strives to seduce her. The ending, which praises remorse of conscience and the married life, is typical of Tamayo's plays. The duke repents his crime, swears that the married woman has not surrendered her honor, and leaves with dignity. Husband and wife are reunited.

VI   Don Simplicio Bobadilla, *1853*

Tamayo and his actor brother Victorino called this play *Don Simplicio Bobadilla,* "a musical drama (*zarzuela*)[12] with magic." Its plot, which is subordinate to the spectacle, includes nymphs, the god Pan, satyrs, a necromancer, a masked ball, birds that talk, and many other fantastic things.

In the play, Pan and his satyrs help the fool, Don Simplicio Bobadilla,[13] in his efforts to seduce the beautiful Leonor. She, on the other hand, is protected by the nymphs, who also have powers of enchantment, and both sides play tricks on each other. A charming sorceress sent by Pan seduces Leonor's husband and Leonor is jealous, but the nymphs keep Don Simplicio from approaching her. By magical art, they finally put him in a cage surrounded by wild beasts. The bailiffs must come to rescue him. Then the scene changes to a quixotic inn where the women have names like Dorotea and Maritornes. Dorotea, the foolish, fickle sister of the innkeeper, who loves to tell tales from the novels of chivalry, is attracted to Don Simplicio. One by one, all the characters of the play come to the inn.

After a great deal of intrigue, there is a brawl at the inn and the water nymphs hasten to rescue Leonor. Pan no longer helps Don Simplicio because he has fallen in love with a nymph who makes him do her bidding. A huge hen swallows Simplicio and when Dorotea blows a magic whistle and asks where he is, a sign appears saying, "In the kingdom of the birds." At the end Dorotea frees Simplicio from a huge egg, after he promises to marry her. Leonor is reunited with her husband, and the chorus sings an exemplary ending:

> The peace of a spouse
> hoping to disturb,

Don Simplicio suffered
punishment superb.

Tran-Tran and *Don Simplicio Bobadilla* offer a lot of spectacle,
and *An Adventure of Richelieu* offers a fast-moving plot filled
with intrigue. Such plays delighted audiences in the 1850's, and
Tamayo took pleasure in accommodating them. As a young man
he was bent on entertainment, although the seeds of moralization were budding forth here and there.[14]

CHAPTER 7

The Aesthetics of Tamayo

I The Speech to the Royal Academy

ON June 12, 1859, Tamayo read his reception speech before the Spanish Royal Academy of Language.[1] Outside of being chosen by the academicians, this speech was the only formal requirement for membership.

Tamayo had been elected to the Academy on March 18, 1858. Since he was singularly young for such an honor, the highest to which a Spanish man of letters might aspire, he was anxious to read his speech and become an active member.[2] He wrote no plays during the period after his election, but spent long hours considering the problems of aesthetics. He wrote and rewrote his ideas until he felt they were fit to be heard by the greatest authors and most learned men of Spain. Finally, on the appointed day, he was ready to deliver them in public.

The Academy speeches of the mid-nineteenth century generally fell into three parts. First, an assertion of humility and gratitude, by which the author referred to his own scant merits and thanked the Academy for overlooking them and admitting him. Second, a tribute to the deceased member, whose chair the reader of the speech was to occupy. And third, the main topic of the speech, the original subject the new academician had chosen to talk about.

In one page,[3] Tamayo succinctly addressed himself to parts one and two of his speech. His attitude was formal but not perfunctory when he said:

On presenting myself before the Spanish Royal Academy, on an occasion that is and will always be the highest and most solemn of my entire public life, in vain do I seek counsel from cold reason, aid and strength from the imperious nature of the circumstances. . . . I at your side in this place? I the peer of sages and worthy men?

97

I the companion of those who have gloriously grown old in a long career? (*OC*, 1133)

In the mouth of another orator words like these might be only a formality, but for Tamayo entrance ito the Academy was an event so cherished it constituted a new citizenship. His naturalization as a chair-holding member was in truth "the highest and most solemn occasion of my entire public life," and, now twenty-nine, he was indeed the companion of men "gloriously grown old." The Academy meant so much to him, he had spent fifteen long months preparing the acceptance speech.[4]

Tamayo then offers a eulogy of the deceased member:

And if in the place I come to occupy I imagine I can still see the worthy academician Don Juan González Cabo-Reluz, at one time the teacher of our august queen; theologian and man of letters; and venerable for his great age; sacred for his priestly character; how do I not withdraw in fear? How do I not doubt that I ought never to place my sights on something so lofty? I confess, candidly, . . . I was unable to resist the influence of a century in which no one knows how to wait. (*OC*, 1133)

Here again there is hyperbole, but for a man of Tamayo's day his rhetoric is justifiable. It is in keeping with his own character and his philosophy of "God, King and Country." For him the queen, the rightful heir to the throne of St. Ferdinand, is really august; a theologian is much above other men; old age—to be sure, anything traditional—is venerable; a priest has a sacred character according to the law of Melchizedec, and a man (Tamayo, and the traditionalists of his day) does stand in awe of these things. Furthermore, the nineteenth century, which Tamayo often excoriates in his plays, is in fact speeding up change. It is a time of extreme impatience.

After complimenting the Academy and its deceased member, Tamayo indicates the subject matter of his speech. He will speak of "truth, considered as the source of beauty in dramatic literature" (*OC*, 1134).

II   *Truth, The Source of Beauty in Dramatic Literature*

Tamayo argues that the finding of truth (*lo verdadero*) is an imperious necessity for the intellect, in all its operations. The intellect is unable to act otherwise. It behooves science to investigate the truth (*la verdad*) as a positive fact; it behooves philosophy to analyze it as a pure abstraction; and it behooves the arts to represent it as a sensible reality. Science and philosophy are not more interested in the truth than the arts; they differ from the arts only in their mode of finding it.

Tamayo now restricts his argument to the arts. Some arts, architecture and music, for example, cannot fulfill the end of the intellect (the finding of truth), because they take only "formless elements" from reality (*OC*, 1134). This does not mean that other arts cannot imitate nature, arts receiving "completed forms" from her (*OC*, 1135). Such arts are sculpture, painting, and poetry.

There is a hierarchy among the arts. Of all the arts, poetry is supreme because of its all-embracing word. No other art can arrive as she does at the manifestation of the moral[5] world. But within poetry itself there is a gradation, with dramatic poetry at the crown. Lyrical poetry sings the affections of the soul; epic poetry narrates the diverse fortunes of the hero; but only dramatic poetry represents the integral and living person. Moreover, in dramatic poetry the author disappears and the play's characters exist in their own persons, free of an outside will and in full enjoyment of their own will. They function on their own, they speak for themselves, they alone reveal themselves. They become on the stage real and actual flesh, and thus "nature becomes an instrument of art" (*OC*, 1135); that is to say, truth becomes an instrument of beauty. Tamayo uses the words "nature" and "reality" as synonyms and at times he uses "truth" as a near-synonym.[6]

The key words in Tamayo's dramatic theory are the following: *realidad, naturaleza* (reality, nature); *imitar, reproducir, representar* (to imitate, to reproduce, to represent); and *forma* (form). They are repeated over and over again in his speech. According to Tamayo, "God is the only creator" (*OC*, 1135).[7] Reality, or nature, comes from Him, and no one else can bring a new world into being, not even an artistic genius. An artist, strictly speaking, does not create a fictitious figure but rather fashions it "in the image and likeness of the living creature" (*OC*, 1135). Thus art is mimetic: it imitates reality (nature). This means that the source of beauty in dramatic literature is truth, since truth by definition is the correspondence of something to reality.[8]

The question arises of the manner of imitation. How does a playwright perceive reality so that he can make his dramatic figures conform to it and so produce[9] a work of art? At this point Tamayo introduces his idea of sensible forms.[10] Man is a Proteus of innumerable forms (*OC*, 1140-41). Men are identical in their being, but unique in their mode of being; each will be recognized as a distinct subject by his changeable form (*OC*, 1138). The artist ought to:

> . . . carefully select, from amongst the elements which appear joined and mixed in reality, only those worthy of appearing in art; elements whose sensible form he will strip of imperfect and useless traits, and of whose invisible essence he will reproduce only what is intimate and precious, so that it may shine forth through that sensible form. . . . Art is a crucible in which the gold is separated from the dross; art is a bee that takes honey from flowers; it is a glass in which the rays of the sun gather and burn. (*OC*, 1137)

This passage is important. The "invisible essence" of man is his soul. The soul itself is not the form of which Tamayo speaks; he speaks rather of manifestations (*OC*, 1134, 1135, 1141) of the soul, such as love, generosity, gratitude, filial piety, loyalty, and hate, greed, ingratitude, prodigality, and disloyalty, all of which are Tamayesque forms of the soul. It behooves the dramatic artist to strip these manifestations of their dross so that the spectator may apprehend them and enjoy them. The "invisible essence," the soul itself, will shine forth through these forms and the spectator will profit by them.[11] This argument is readily acceptable in the case of virtues; but even a vice such as hate, as long as it is treated as a means to an end and not an end in itself, can lead to the true and beautiful; such a vice is worthy of being reproduced, represented, imitated. The ugly is permissible in art; nay, it is desirable, as long as it is treated as a means to an end (*OC*, 1140, 1143).

Up to this point, Tamayo has been giving his theory of "truth, considered as the source of beauty in dramatic literature." Now, he says, he will turn from theory to experience. He will give examples in support of his theory. Both the ancient theater and the modern, both the classical theater and the romantic, will show how truth (*lo verdadero*) has always been the determining quality of beauty (*lo bello*).

What was there in pagan antiquity? Gods made in the likeness of man, with the same passions and needs. And what was there on earth? Men, says Tamayo, with souls imprisoned in the jail of their flesh. The soul could not function without the aid of the senses, and so it was enslaved. And governing heaven and earth there was a blind will that was so absurd it did not even know itself. Thus, the human and the divine were confused into one, and matter and spirit were bound tightly together. Men had no individual liberty, they were absorbed by the state, they did not know the family, they looked on women only as a means of pleasure. This was the civilization that the pagan drama faithfully portrayed (it faithfully imitated the manifestations of the soul, the forms, that were evident at that time).

A faithful portrayal of this pagan world is Oedipus. The blind instrument of destiny, he cannot overcome the preestablished order. He cannot become excited and stir himself with the passionate defiance of individual existence. He cannot bring his humanity to its full development. Nevertheless, let us contemplate him rejecting with the wrath of an innocent man the charges brought against him; striving all the more to ascertain his evil fortune the more clear it becomes; doubting what he does not want to believe; anxiously seizing on the slightest hope; surrendering to the evidence before him and longing for his own punishment; looking with horror on his children; impetuously rising up when others try to take them from him. In short, let us contemplate Oedipus, human and true, and as such pathetic and great. *Oedipus Rex* is a beautiful drama because it is true to ancient Greece and the men of that time[12] (*OC*, 1147-48).

According to Tamayo, the difference between the ancient drama and the modern is the difference between paganism and Christianity. The ancient drama is like a serene lake contained within a border of flowers; its waters are crystal clear but not deep. The modern theater, which comes after the Incarnate Word, revealed the abyss separating heaven and earth; it is like the sea, never completely at rest, apparently borderless, which denies to the eyes, but not to the soul, its great depths and the

riches hidden there. Ancient man was predictable, modern man
is not, and this fact affects the form of the modern theater, which
Tamayo calls "romantic":

The narrow bed of the ancient tragedy will be too narrow for . . .
the combined action of free will and Providence, for the enraptured
flight of the soul toward the infinite; these require the wide open
field of the romantic scene. Similarly, the cult of the true God could
not fit into the limited pagan temple, but required the spacious
cathedral with its labyrinth of naves and columns. (*OC*, 1150)

The modern theater was the undertaking of "those priest poets"
of "our own Spain"[13] and of that most forceful Englishman,
Shakespeare.[14]

Tamayo maintains that the romantic form triumphed over
the classic form because it is "truer" than the latter. By this he
means that nature is varied and the romantic form is varied,
whereas the classic form is not enlivened by variety. But there
is also the question of content. In nature we find "the good and
all that which constitutes a general rule"; nature does not con-
centrate on what is evil or exceptional. Therefore, the playwright with his romantic form[15] should present (or re-present)
what is good and constitutes a general rule; he should not con-
centrate on the evil or exceptional.[16]

Tamayo then refers to many authors. The works of Calderón,
Lope, Rojas, Moreto, Tirso, Ruiz de Alarcón, Shakespeare, Cor-
neille, Racine, Molière, Schiller, and Moratín will all bear out
his argument. They were great dramatists because they painted
scenes "with brushes stolen from nature" (*OC*, 1154).

Tamayo finally turns to the drama of the nineteenth century.
Many will condemn it, he says, or many will praise it unthink-
ingly. He will fall into neither extreme. He will not praise "its
blameworthy errors," neither will he overlook its "noteworthy
beauties" (*OC*, 1154). He lauds the Duke of Rivas' *Don Álvaro* and Hartzenbusch's *The Lovers of Teruel*. They strike a
chord in the Christian soul. Of *Don Álvaro* he says:

When you see him cast himself from the rock into the abyss, is your
soul not troubled wondering if eternal condemnation awaits him?
Do you not like to think that in one instant, as he falls, repentance
can save him? Thus the Christian drama brings the mind of the

creature to the Creator, although the outcome is never verified on earth, but in heaven. (*OC*, 1155)

Tamayo concludes his speech with his original idea, that truth is the source of beauty in dramatic literature. He also adds the concept of the good:

Art will achieve its ends only when the beautiful, the true and the good are united in it, like tender brothers. Only then will art be the noble delight and sure mover of hearts, the instruction of nations, the companion of philosophy, the well-loved child of religion, the worthy calling of the spirit that the Supreme Maker gave us; the spirit that has in its creative faculty a sure pledge of immortality. (*OC*, 1164)

III   A Critique of Tamayo's Aesthetics

In his scheme of mimetic dramatic art, Tamayo uses the word *forma,* or form, in two different ways without spelling out the difference between them. First he uses *forma* as something that will enter the content of a drama, whereas later he uses *forma* to mean the style or technique of a drama, the container of the content.[17] Other Spanish critics speak of meaning and form (*sentido y forma*) or substance and form (*fondo y forma*), but Tamayo speaks of form and form.[18] Obviously the use of one word with two different meanings is apt to confuse Tamayo's reader.

Tamayo's first *forma,* what we might call the active, substantive form, is the more important of the two *formas.* It exists in nature, which precedes art:

... architecture and music, they do not take from reality anything except elements without form—from this one should not conclude that other arts ought not to imitate nature, arts which receive completed forms, so to speak, such as sculpture, painting and poetry. (*OC*, 1134-35)

Tamayo's first *forma,* or active form, is similar to Aristotle's substantial form in the latter's theory of hylomorphism.[19] According to Tamayo, architects and musicians practice an inferior art because they work with something that is passive and formless, something like the Aristotelian prime matter. Sculptors, painters, and poets, on the other hand, work with a higher, determining, active substance, called form. In the case of the dramatic poet, this form (or these forms) is the manifestation of the human soul whose actions he, with his all-embracing word, can capture better than anyone else. Therefore, his art is superior.

In his use of this Aristotelian form, Tamayo exercises a license that modern thinkers find confusing. He applies the word *forma* not only to the psyche itself, but also to all the operations of the psyche, to its passions and even to its evil activity.[20] Thus the forms the poet will "take from the true and the real" (that is, from nature)[21] include "the hidden incentives of the will," "the most impenetrable operations of the conscience," "the deepest depths of the mind and heart." If the poet takes these things from nature and his name happens to be Shakespeare, he will produce characters like Lady Macbeth, Juliet, Desdemona, Shylock, Richard III, Macbeth, Othello, Romeo, Hamlet, and Lear (*OC*, 1153). In Tamayo's aesthetics, the soul of a man gives forth manifestations that are forms: his love is a form, his jealousy is a form. If the poet imitates these, he may create an Othello, who will appear to have a true soul vivifying him (*OC*, 1153).

Simply put, Tamayo says that a playwright must look at nature and there he will see a woman with womanhood, a mother with motherhood, a daughter with daughterhood, an orphan with orphanhood, a man with manhood, a swain with swainhood, a father with fatherhood, a miser with miserliness, a coward with cowardice, a liar with false witness, a murderer with murder in his heart, a lecher with lechery, a saint with sainthood, a hero with heroism. He will see the various virtues, vices, passions, and states incarnate in good men and bad. The playwright must study men, absorb the forms in them, and imitate the forms in the characters of his own dramas not in a servile way, but with "the utmost freedom" (*con libérrima acción*), *OC*, 1136. The artist's "utmost freedom" will never lead to disorder because in nature, which is God's creation, the saint will necessarily achieve salvation, the murderer will not.

In one passage Tamayo shows how the playwright can arrive at "the hidden incentives of the will," "the deepest impenetrable operations of the conscience," and "the deepest depths of the mind and heart." In this passage he attaches the adjective *sensible* to the word *forma*. He writes:

Art must select after careful examination, from among the elements which appear mixed together in reality, only those that are worthy of appearing in art: elements whose sensible form it will cleanse of imperfect and useless traits, and of whose invisible essence it will reproduce only what is most intimate and precious; so that the invisible essence may shine forth through that form, like a trimmed light through a lamp glass without stain. (*OC*, 1137)

In other words, forms, which are in themselves invisible and impalpable, appear in a world of matter, which is visible and palpable. Matter makes the forms *sensibles,* that is, capable of being sensed. The poet must go beyond appearances, beyond "the imperfect and useless," and extract "the invisible essence." One might think that the invisible essence is the form itself,[22] but Tamayo separates the two. Now, by his power of imitation, the dramatic poet can purge the form of its dross and put it into his fictitious character so that the invisible essence can shine forth. The audience will apprehend the cleansed form and see the essence shining through it, much as it would see a light shining through a spotless glass.[23]

In his argument thus far, Tamayo has said that the manifestations of the soul of a dramatic figure, e.g., Othello, are an imitation of the manifestations of the soul of a real man. This imitation is the foundation stone of Tamayo's aesthetics. According to him, it is the content of the theater.[24]

Elsewhere in his argument, however, Tamayo uses the word *forma* in a completely different way. He is not referring to the content of dramatic art, but to its container, its style, its technique, its mode of re-presentation, its use of verse or prose, its use or disuse of the unities of time, action, and place, its plots, its scenery and costumes; in brief, to the vessel an artist pours his content into. And so Tamayo writes:

See then, gentlemen, how the triumph of the romantic form over the classic form, always and everywhere, is owing to the fact that the former is more true than the latter. (*OC*, 1151)

In his Academy speech, Tamayo has been associating Romanticism with Christianity. The classic theater, he says, was re-

stricted because man was restricted. Man lived under fate. But
Christ's coming liberated man because it insisted on his free
will. This gave human life a tremendous variety. The classic
form (the three unities, for example) suited a man of fate, but
the romantic form, which permits much more diversity, suits
a man of free will. According to Tamayo, Shakespeare, Calderón,
and Schiller are all of them Romantics.

A diagram may help the reader to understand Tamayo's two
uses of the word *forma*:

Tamayo's Usage

I. *Forma*: it is similar to Aristotle's substantial form. The content
of the theater is the imitation of, the re-presentation of, this *forma* on
the stage. This *forma* is, so to speak, the soul of art. (The *forma
sensible* is what an artist can perceive in his fellowman.) In brief,
this *forma* is the content.

II. *Forma*: Classic form or romantic form. The style, the technique.
The mode of presenting the content above. This second *forma* must
imitate the metaphysical or quasi-metaphysical form above. In brief,
this *forma* is the container. The container is subordinate to the content.

In Tamayo, I takes precedence over II.

Common Usage Today

I. *Fondo* or *sentido*: the substance of a play, the meaning of a
play, the subject matter. What the author says. In brief, this *fondo* or
sentido is the content.

II. *Forma*: the form. The form that the artist gives to the content.
The poet's word or *logos*. This *forma* is often considered to be the
very soul of art. The poet's word informs the *fondo* or *sentido*. In
brief, the container. The content is subordinate to the container.[25]

Here, Tamayo's position is reversed. II takes precedence over I.

Thus in Tamayo's system, the content comes first. The mimesis
consists of the form's imitating the *forma,* or content. The poet's
word is not so much a *logos*, which breathes spirit into a poem,
as a mirror reflecting a higher light. In common usage today, on
the other hand, the poet's work is a *logos*, a sort of divine inspira-

tion, which breathes life into an otherwise formless content. For Tamayo the artist is a procreator, a mimetic man, a person who should imitate the Savior, Christ. For many modern critics, the artist is rather like a priest, a creator, a savior in his own right.[26]

IV *Tamayo's Plays in The Light of His Academy Speech*

In some respects, Tamayo's plays and the Academy speech are of one and the same piece. Both are concerned with man, and above man, with God. Both emphasize the question of good and evil, with good as an end, triumphant in the long run, and evil as a persistent adversary that must finally lose. Both his plays and his speech look upon the human body and other material objects as something to be deprecated, even scorned, and the soul as a spirit that always longs for its final resting place, which it can achieve after death. Both refer to eternal salvation or damnation. Both rely at times on the same kind of rhetoric, in which one speaks of "degenerate beings," "deformities of the soul," "vile instincts," "terrible passions," "horrendous desperation," 'infamous thirst"; and these rhetorical expressions are clustered around the thought that something material will "adulterate" or "prostitute" something spiritual. In summary, Tamayo's plays and the Academy speech both point to the thought that God has created man, who is entirely dependent on Him and must seek Him by fleeing all the things of this world, including his own body. Tamayo is the popularizer of a rather stern theology.

Nevertheless, Tamayo's Academy speech is not all theology; as we have seen, he advances a doctrine of imitable forms, which the artist can perceive in nature. It behooves the critical reader to see how well he put his own doctrines into practice.

In the Academy speech, Tamayo frequently makes statements such as the following:

This fictitious creature [of drama], to be beautiful, must be formed in the image and likeness of the living creature. (*OC*, 1135)

The scenic fiction will cease to be beautiful and will sin moreover on the side of falsehood, when it represents the unusual and the unnatural, the exception and not the rule. (*OC*, 1136)

One mineral differs little from another; a plant will differ from
another plant more than that; and even more, one brute from
another. And by reason of the free exercise of his moral potencies,
each man, in his mode of being, differs radically from other men.
(*OC*, 1137)

But if the figure is arbitrarily realized by the poet (and in no other
way can abstractions be realized), he will have to adopt, necessarily,
a unique and petrified form. Without such a form, the same figure
will be reproduced each and every time, and it will differ in no
way from its fellow creatures ... it will be monotonous, like the
copy put out by the daguerreotype a hundred times over. (*OC*, 1138)

Those figures who aspire to be pure spirit, pure heroism, pure goodness, will not be spiritual, or heroic, or good; with an air of being
supernatural, they will be worth a thousand times less than nature;
they will cause surprise perhaps, they will never stir the emotions.
(*OC*, 1140)

The reader who applies these standards of Tamayo to his
dramas will have to judge many of these harshly. Tamayo's
fictitious characters are frequently not artistic because they are
not "formed in the image and likeness of the living creature";
they are, moreover, "unusual and unnatural, the exception and
not the rule." In *The Snowball*, for example, characters like
Clara and Luis change their minds too quickly and too often.
They have displayed an unusual jealousy, which is a wooden
attitude with them, rather than a deeply felt passion, and at the
end they suddenly exclaim:

CLARA. Make her happy, my God!
LUIS. Eternal God, make him happy!

In fashioning the characters of Clara and Luis, Tamayo did
not observe the vital forms he professed to see about him;
rather the forms, or their dramatic imitators, are rigid.

Tamayo says that one mineral differs little from another. He
also says that a petrified form is necessary for the arbitrary
realization of abstractions. In his own terms, then, it must be
said that the figures in his dramas, especially his moral theater,
behave like minerals and have a petrified air. They do not
change.[27] Doña Candelaria of *Duels of Honor* is virtually the

same person as Fabian of *The Upright Men*. Both are the *raison-neur*, the person who steps aside here and there in the play to point out a moral. One can see a similar petrification in the young man who suddenly inherits a fortune and marries a poor girl, an orphan, or a girl with a bad father (*The Snowball, The Right Track*); or in the bad man who is suddenly converted at the end (*Duels of Honor, The Snowball, Daughter and Mother, Every Evil Hath Its Good*). The denunciations of wealth, of modern industry, of ingratitude, of heresy, of irreligion, of sin, are all of them cast a hundred times from the same monotonous daguerreotype. They are not lifelike. It can also be said that too many of Tamayo's characters aspire to be pure spirit; with their supernatural yearnings, they cease to conform to nature. They do not differ one from the other. "They will cause surprise perhaps; they will never stir the emotions."

On the other hand, in those plays or scenes where Tamayo follows the pronouncements of his Academy speech, he writes at his best. Such pieces are *A New Drama, The Madness of Love, Doña Juana the Magnate*, the first two acts of *Every Evil Hath Its Good*, the second act of *Duels of Honor*, and the short comedies, *A Wager, Out of the Frying Pan*, and *Cunning Rather Than Force*.

If we accept Tamayo's doctrine of forms, it would seem at times that he perceived them as being more rigid and unvaried than they really are, and at other times that he perceived them as being much more flexible, that is to say, the way they are in reality. His rigid vision can be found in his moral theater, where he proposes to teach (*enseñar*); whereas his flexible vision can be seen in the dramas that propose to please (*deleitar*) the audience.

In brief, when Tamayo is preaching virtue he does not follow his own aesthetics. When he is not preaching virtue but writes to entertain, he is more apt to follow them. Unfortunately, he chose to preach a good deal of the time.[28]

CHAPTER 8

Conclusion

MANUEL Tamayo y Baus (1829-1898) lived and wrote in a Spain that had not for the most part accepted liberalism and the industrial revolution. A traditionalist whose motto was "God, King and Country," he placed his conservative ideas in almost all his theater. It is historically significant that he died in 1898, the year of Spain's war with the United States, for his death also symbolizes the passing of an old order. Tamayo had to disappear, as it were, before Unamuno and other young writers of the day could bring a new Spanish essence (*casticismo*) to Spanish literature.

Tamayo represented logic, law, stability, constancy, and order, qualities usually associated with reason. Indeed, he was a man of reason who saw a unity in Spain dating back to St. Ferdinand, the Cid, and ancient Rome. He was also a man of religion who saw the central point of history in the Incarnation of Jesus Christ. Rational and religious, he did not have the gift of lyricism. He could argue the praises of Spain and its God, but he could not sing them. Thus he stood in contrast to the young men of 1898, wonderfully gifted writers, who assailed reason, and sometimes religion, and sang the praises of the will.

Tamayo's theater more often than not was moral. He wrote plays with a Manichaean tendency, in which modern material success is scorned in favor of ancient values, such as the family, filial duty, charity towards the poor, love of country, and the nobility of women. The most famous of these moral plays are representative of the *alta comedia* (high comedy), which contains a language allegedly higher and more sober than that of the Romantic playwrights; they also concern the upper middle class, those citizens of the nineteenth century who were building railroads, speculating in land, directing banks, and running factories. Tamayo's *alta comedia* paints an unfavorable picture

110

of this middle class, largely because of its vulgarity in handling money. He seems to be telling us that he objects to the new capitalists on three grounds: they are un-Spanish, un-Catholic, and ungentlemanly.

Not everything, however, was morality in Tamayo's theater. He was a master of stagecraft, and he instinctively knew that the purpose of good theater is to entertain the public. Consequently he wrote short comedies, historical dramas, a tragedy, and a play inspired by Shakespeare to delight his audience; he also adapted many plays from the French stage. Of all his plays, the universal favorite has been *A New Drama*, in which the world of flesh-and-blood men and the world of the theater are blended into one.

Tamayo also wrote a discourse on aesthetics, which he read before his beloved Royal Academy of Language. Here he included the idea that filled every corner of his life: "Men, and above men, God." He also expounded a neo-Aristotelian doctrine of art. He argued for naturalness in the theater rather than contrivance, and he insisted that characters should have a will of their own and speak for themselves rather than for the author. Had he lived up to his own doctrine, he might have written many more fine plays. Unfortunately he did not, and this accounts for the wooden quality of so many of the works he did write.

Tamayo was an old-fashioned man who erected no wall between church and state, or between art, church, and state. He saw everything as one, *sub specie aeternitatis*. His most fitting epitaph is the last sentence of his prologue to *Ángela*:

Faith will provide where the intelligence is wanting. (*OC*, 154)

Appendix 1

The Carlist Letter

Chapter 1 refers to this letter, which Tamayo wrote when he decided to run for public office on the Carlist platform. This was an open letter, addressed to his electorate:

Does the liberal monarchy please you? Take a good look at it. The heresy of Luther triumphant over the Catholic Church; religious unity taken away from all Spaniards for the benefit of a few Protestants or atheists, who being atheists or Protestants, are not Spaniards though they were born in Spain; the liberty of evil applauded and recognized and for that very reason the liberty of good denied and struck down, because good men and bad men cannot be free at one and the same time; power, exercised in the name of reason, rebelling against faith, the insufferable and barbarous tyranny of man over man. The means of repression? These two exclusively: insidious corruption and brutal force. The law of equity? Only one: to give everything to a friend, to deny everything to an adversary. As a permanent system of government, the division and enmity of Spaniards, whose blood will flow endlessly, shed by a Spanish hand in infamous battles, so that both conquerors and vanquished will share equally in the mourning and shame. At all times the suffering of horrendous evils, and when not suffering them, the rightful fearing of still greater ones. The public Treasury, without means of attending to the most urgent necessities, weighed down by an insufferable debt and with the slogan of *waste ahead,* more and more resolved to keep working for the ruin not only of this generation, but also of future generations, as long as there is no curtailment of the enormous expenses necessary for the functioning of the enormous machine of liberalism. Intrigue, calumny, force, lies, these are the best arms for political combat; vileness, the key to scandalous success; peculation, offering itself boldly to public admiration; every crime, crowned with the laurel of virtue or the palm of heroism. Wherever you will, towns and families without happiness or repose; perverted minds, hearts filled with corruption, souls in despair. On all sides, impiety, injustice, sorrow, misery, opprobrium. And as a consolation for so many ills, not even one lone ray of glory, no

113

hope of remedy; and as a final consequence and clear proof of the
benefits which the fatherland owes to the liberal spirit that animates
it for so many years now, the Spanish throne, which St. Ferdinand
held, occupied now by a foreigner; on the throne of a saint, the
son of Victor Immanuel. This is liberal Spain. Does it please you:
Then vote for him who says: I am a liberal, and consequently, a
supporter of Amadeus I. Do you prefer the Catholic Monarchy?
The Monarchy that, embracing the Church of Jesus Christ, governs
in the name of eternal principles; that is not free to contaminate and
much less to suppress; imposing on men not the yoke of another
man, but the most sweet and holy yoke of the truth and the justice
that come from God, by which rule is legitimate and obedience easy,
and both rule and obedience are jointly ennobled and exalted? That
not only gives liberty to the good, but also help and encouragement,
and not only does not recognize the rights of evil, but also even
denies it the right of existence? That far from establishing the life
of the State on the perpetual and fratricidal war of the parties,
hopes to establish it on the union of all Spaniards beneath the flag
of one common sentiment and one universal belief? That rewards
and punishes according to the law and not for a selfish reason or
tyrannical whim? That brings about through paternal love, peace,
and the good fortune of towns and families, clipping the wings of
irreligion which poisons everything? That corrects the incredible
abuses of the civil service, the principal cause of the lamentable
state of our Treasury, in favor of social order and the stability of
Government, new sources of public wealth, to the benefit of industry,
commerce, and the arts? Do you prefer the Catholic Monarchy, the
kind that can only be established today by its one legitimate and
true representative in Spain, DON CARLOS DE BORBÓN Y ESTE,
for whose legal triumph his supporters should overlook no licit
means? In that case vote for me. I say to you: "I am a Catholic
and therefore a Carlist."

MANUEL TAMAYO Y BAUS°

° The Spanish original of this letter can be found in Ramón Esquer
Torres, "Tamayo y Baus y la Política del Siglo XIX," *Segismundo: Revista
Hispánica de Teatro,* I (1965), 71-91.

Appendix 2

The Letter to Don Carlos de Borbón

Appendix 1 contains a letter, written in the spring of 1871, from Manuel Tamayo y Baus to the electorate of Santo Domingo de la Calzada. About the same time he addressed a letter to Don Carlos de Borbón, the pretender to the throne:

Sire:

It is true what Your Majesty affirms in the gracious letter with which he has deigned to gladden my heart and give me an unmerited honor: I am in the camp where the beloved banner of Cervantes and Calderón is raised: the banner in whose shadow Spain outdid in glory and beauty all her brothers, the other nations, children of the Cross.

As for the principles and ideas of religion and government, Divine Mercy has always kept me in the same camp. That is why, earlier, when the throne was not vacant, and although I had performed no political act, I owed the name of *neo-Catholic* to the liberals: that is why I now take the name of Carlist.

Your Majesty says, let the Truth rise to the throne with me. So be it, we Spanish Catholics say, and let the king rule in us: the Truth in the king.

There are many today who ask the same question as Pilate. Well and good, let them ask it, since it is not possible, unfortunately, to send men to school where they might learn Christian doctrine. Your Majesty and we others, we know what the *Truth* is.

Consequently I have very strong reasons for wanting to see the crown of St. Ferdinand on your brow; and such must be the desire, to my way of thinking, of every Spaniard who truly loving God loves his country.

Every noble and pious Spaniard who today sees God crucified in Spain and in Him his country itself; who cannot satisfy his conscience by merely fulfilling private duties or by defending Catholicism as a pure abstraction in ideal regions; every noble and pious Spaniard who today feels obligated to enter the political arena, in the hope of procuring there, by practical means and results, the positive triumph of religion over official atheism and of good government

115

over the tyrannical rule of anarchy; such a Spaniard must inevitably and necessarily elect one of two paths: (1) either embrace the cause of Your Majesty or (2) contribute, although unwillingly, to the fact that the monstrous abortion of Lutheran heresy, abominated by the Church, and with it liberalism, will continue to rule in Spain now with all their shamelessness and barbarism, now with their forms hypocritical and smooth; the latter, perhaps the most efficacious for the liberal work of corrupting honorable breasts and pure souls, of frustrating the supreme end and the earthly happiness of man and of bringing the social body to a frightful death; the social body, all of it in wounds, all of it prostrate in the face of infamous corruption and ignominious putrefaction.

Because now, sire, none of the political parties that reject you and seek the rule of Spain, and can win it, none of them fails to boast of its liberal title, and to say "liberal" is to say "adversary of Catholicism" in government and in social order; because now in Spain there is only one political denomination which is different from or contrary to the liberal one: namely, the Carlist party, which means the party in favor of Catholic government and an ordered society.

To establish the rule of justice, which means the absolute dominion of good over evil; to destroy and annihilate the impious state founded against all divine law and every natural right in a Catholic people; to do these things, then, we call on Your Majesty, we who follow your banner; we call on you to save Spain once more, as her ancient kings have saved her in the past. They had to reconquer Spain for God: for God Your Majesty must reconquer her; they, against Mohammed; Your Majesty, against Luther.

Oh great joy and even greater responsibility! Tremendous, frightening, ineffable responsibility, that of the man in whom a people sees its leader, providentially destined to redeem it from captivity and to make it free and perhaps the eminent guiding light of other nations in the world, today lost once again in the darkness of error, shipwrecked today in a stormy sea of blood and tears!

No infamy is comparable to the infamy that might await such a man: not even the infamy of a King born of liberalism: on the other hand, his glory might even outdo that of Recaredo* or Pelayo.**

This laurel, which Your Majesty dreams of, will one day adorn your brow if God hears the prayers of Spanish Catholics.

May He guard Your Majesty,
From Your Majesty's most respectful subject,

Manuel   Tamayo   y   Baus

* Recaredo I, King of the Visigoths, 586-601. A convert to Catholicism, his reign represents the triumph of Catholic Spain over Arian Spain, that is, the destruction of heresy and the victory of the true faith.

**Pelayo, King of Asturias, 718-737. The leader of the Asturian rebellion against the Moslems, his name represents the Reconquest, that is, the victory of the Cross over the Crescent.

Notes and References

Chapter One

1. See H. Chonon Berkowitz, *Pérez Galdós, Spanish Liberal Crusader* (Madison: University of Wisconsin Press, 1948).
2. The reader will find a translation of this letter in Appendix 1. He will find a translation of a private letter from Tamayo to Carlos de Borbón, whom the Carlists called Carlos VII, Duque de Madrid, in Appendix 2.
3. See Tamayo's necrology by E. Cotarelo y Mori, in *Revista de Archivos, Bibliotecas y Museos*, II (July, 1898), 289.
4. Strictly speaking, Tamayo's first play was *Genoveva de Brabante* (*Genevieve of Brabant*), which was staged by his parents when he was eleven years old. Tamayo's friend, Aureliano Fernández-Guerra, described the occasion in a speech given in 1858, in which he welcomed Tamayo into the Royal Academy. See Aureliano Fernández-Guerra y Orbe, "Discurso de contestación," in *Discursos leídos en las recepciones públicas que ha celebrado desde 1847 la Real Academia Española*, Tomo Segundo (Madrid, 1860), 293-94. And see the necrology of E. Cotarelo y Mori, *op. cit.*, 291-92. Scholars have failed to find a copy of *Genoveva de Brabante*.
5. In his necrology of Tamayo, E. Cotarelo y Mori has this to say of Victorino: "The eminent actor D. Victorino, who so brilliantly supported his brother playing the roles in some of his works, above all that of Yorick in *A New Drama*, in such a way that its equal has not been seen since." *Op. cit.*, 291.
6. In this letter, Tamayo is writing in his official capacity as Secretary of the Royal Academy. See Ramón Esquer Torres, "Para un Epistolario Tamayo y Baus—Menéndez Pelayo," in *Boletín de la Biblioteca de Menéndez y Pelayo*, Tomo 38 (1962), 158-59.
7. I translate the entire letter in order to give the reader some idea of Tamayo's humor while Secretary of the Royal Academy (1874-1898). Tamayo is often presented as a staid man, but in fact his letters show a sense of fun. Apparently, his work as Secretary had its humorous side; for example, the poet José Zorrilla (1817-1893), who wanted to read one of his legends in verse as his acceptance speech into the Academy, was persuaded to give a more conventional speech instead. And so Zorrilla read his speech . . . in

verse. See the *Boletín de la Real Academia,* Tomo 39 (1959), 96.

8. Tamayo's personal copy of Hegel, preserved today in the Academy's library, is the French edition *La poétique,* Paris, 1855. See Egon Schwarz, "Manuel Tamayo y Baus y Schiller," in *Comparative Literature,* XIII (1961), 129-30.

9. See Ramón Esquer Torres, "Tamayo y Baus y la Real Academia Española," in the *Boletín de la Real Academia,* Tomo 43 (1962), 309. According to the testimony of Isidoro Fernández Flórez, Tamayo studied and translated the plays of foreign literatures, including German, from the age of eight on. See R. Esquer Torres, "Epistolario de Manuel Tamayo y Baus a Manuel Cañete," *Revista de Literatura,* XIX (1961), 371. It would appear that Fernández Flórez (Fernanflor) has created a pious legend.

For the letter to Menéndez Pelayo concerning Latin, see R. Esquer Torres, "Para un Epistolario Tamayo y Baus—Menéndez Pelayo," in *Boletín de la Biblioteca de Menéndez Pelayo, op. cit.,* 170. In his letter of April 2, 1844, the fourteen-year-old Tamayo had written: "I'll bet a volume of the *Aeneid* against the speech of any congressman that . . ." This reference to the *Aeneid* may be an image from earlier years and may mean that he had about two years of Latin. See R. Esquer Torres, "Epistolario de Manuel Tamayo y Baus a Manuel Cañete," *op. cit.*

10. See Neale Tayler, *Las fuentes del teatro de Tamayo y Baus* (Madrid, 1959), p. 109. Chapter IV is called "Tamayo y el teatro francés."

11. R. Esquer Torres, "Epistolario de Manuel Tamayo y Baus a Manuel Cañete," *op. cit.,* 371.

12. Villaamil, the protagonist of Benito Pérez Galdós' *Miau,* is a *cesante.* This novel is now available in paperback English translation.

13. I use the word "thesis" here to include all of Tamayo's moralizing theater. In Chapter Two, I draw a distinction between his thesis play, *Lances de honor (Duels of Honor),* and his other plays known as the *alta comedia.*

14. See Narciso Sicars y Salvadó, *D. Manuel Tamayo y Baus, estudio crítico-biográfico* (Barcelona: Tipografía Católica, 1906), p. 50, which lists the extraordinary achievements of Tamayo within the Academy and mentions his "attendance at ordinary sessions which reached the number of 1,950, a figure achieved by no other Academy member." And see R. Esquer Torres, "Tamayo y Baus y la Real Academia Española," in *Boletín de la Real Academia,* Tomo 43 (1962), 315-17.

Incidentally, the chairs in the Academy have an alphabetical arrangement, and Tamayo occupied chair S.

15. The one controversial act of Tamayo as Secretary of the Academy was his opposition to the candidacy of Benito Pérez Galdós, who applied to that corporation for admission. If the reader will examine the letter in Appendix 1 of the present book and read Galdós' novels *Doña Perfecta* and *Gloria,* he will understand the vast gap (the Great Spanish Dichotomy) that lay between the two men. See R. Esquer Torres, "Las luchas del siglo XIX: el P. Blanco García y Leopoldo Alas 'Clarín,' " *Boletín de la Sociedad Castellonense de Cultura,* Tomo 38, Cuaderno 3 (1962), 241-55. Pages 241-43 discuss Tamayo and the candidacy of Galdós. See also H. Chonon Berkowitz, *op. cit.,* 227-35.

16. See R. Esquer Torres, "Tamayo y Baus y la política del XIX," in *Segismundo: Revista Hispánica de Teatro,* I (1965), 82-83. Until the publication of this article in 1965, the critics, following the statement of E. Cotarelo y Mori in his Tamayo necrology of 1898, were wont to say that Tamayo did not engage in politics.

17. I borrow this term from José Ortega y Gasset, who applied it to Pío Baroja's constant stream of insolent words (*improperios*). See José Ortega y Gasset, "Ideas sobre Pío Baroja," and "Una primera vista sobre Pío Baroja," in Ortega's *Obras completas,* II (Madrid, 1963), 69-102 and 103-25.

18. According to Webster's *Third New International Dictionary, Unabridged,* 1967, one meaning of Manichaeanism is this: "a dualistic interpretation of the world, dividing it between good and evil powers or regarding matter as inherently evil." I apply the adjective "Manichaean" to Tamayo in this sense.

19. For an insight into Tamayo's political vision, see the articles of D. L. Shaw listed in the bibliography. Prof. Shaw has pointed out, more profoundly and concisely than any other critic, the metaphysical crisis behind the Spanish Dichotomy.

20. In this passage I am trying to recapture the psychology of Tamayo. Pi y Margall may or may not have been a formal atheist, but that is beside the point. As a heterodox political leader, he is to be classified with atheists and Protestants: this is the way I construe Tamayo's politico-religious vision.

21. In 1863, Ernest Renan published one of the most famous books of the nineteenth century, *The Life of Jesus.* Renan denied that Jesus was God.

22. There is still some confusion over these names. In Appendix I of her unpublished Ph.D. thesis of 1950, Blanche Emma Goodell shows Tamayo using the pseudonym José María García seven times before 1858, and as early as 1853: Blanche Emma Goodell, "Manuel Tamayo y Baus, Sources and Aesthetics," University of Wisconsin

unpublished doctoral dissertation (Madison, 1950), pp. 242-44. On
the other hand, the eminent *tamayista* R. Esquer Torres (*El teatro
de Tamayo y Baus* [Madrid, 1965], p. 149) says that Tamayo first
used pseudonyms after his election into the Academy in 1858. Miss
Goodell, moreover, lists several plays, adaptations from the French,
not mentioned by Esquer Torres or other critics.

23. See "Don Manuel Tamayo y Baus," by Isidoro Fernández
Flórez in Pedro de Novo y Colson, *Autores dramáticos contemporáneos*,
II (Madrid, 1884-1886), 461-86.

24. Tamayo did leave a written testament, but it made no mention
of the destruction of his papers. This part of his will was verbal.
See R. Esquer Torres, "Tamayo y Baus: sus proyectos literarios," in
Boletín de la Real Academia Española, Tomo 43, Cuaderno 168
(enero-abril, 1963), 153.

25. This quotation is from Longfellow's translation of the *Coplas
de Jorge Manrique*, in *The Complete Poetical Works of Henry Wads-
worth Longfellow*, Cambridge Edition (Cambridge, 1922), p. 587.

Chapter Two

1. Four of these plays are known as the *alta comedia*, and the
fifth, *Lances de honor* (*Duels of Honor*), is really a thesis novel set
on the stage. It should be studied alongside the famous thesis novels
of the nineteenth century, Galdós' *Gloria* (1877), Pereda's reply to
Galdós, *De tal palo tal astilla* (1880), Alarcón's *El escándalo* (1875),
Coloma's *Pequeñeces* (1891), and Pérez de Ayala's reply to Coloma,
AMDG (1910). For a study of the *novela de tesis*, see Sherman Eoff,
"The Spanish Novel of Ideas: Critical Opinion (1836-1880)," *PMLA*,
LV (1940), 532-58.

2. The two letters have been translated into English and appear
in Appendix 1 and Appendix 2.

3. In his Academy acceptance speech, Pío Baroja (1872-1956)
has left an interesting note concerning Tamayo: "Some people asked
me why I didn't go to read in the National Library. To be sure,
that center of culture existed in the street now known as Arrieta,
which was then called the Library Street; but they wouldn't let us
have literary books, by order of the director Tamayo y Baus, and in
the end they didn't permit us to read magazines or newspapers
either, because they had serial stories (*folletines*). These prohibitions
ordered by a literary man were comical: a sign of Spanish arbitrari-
ness." See p. 436 of Fernando Baeza, *Baroja y su mundo*, Tomo II
(Madrid, 1961), which reproduces the entire Academy speech. This
passage clearly shows that Tamayo was concerned about the morality

of the young. He was acting as their censor. (I owe this note to my graduate student, Mrs. Jean Batha.)

4. I have translated *Lo positivo* as *The Right Track*, because *lo positivo* is money and when you have money you are on the right track, according to the materialists Tamayo puts in his play. The expression *lo positivo,* which is repeated a score of times in the play, also brings to mind nineteenth-century positivism.

5. In *Lo positivo*, Act I, Scene v, Tamayo divides the body and the soul in such a way that the former seems bad and the latter good: "And so, Cecilia, will you renounce the joys of love for the vile satisfaction of vanity and egoism; the holy joy of the family for the vain pomp of society; the life of the soul for the life of the senses?" (*OC,* 735, 1). For the term Manichaean, see note 18 of Chapter One.

6. The marquis is the uncle of both Cecilia and Rafael, that is, the young lovers are cousins. It was common for cousins to marry in Spanish life and literature.

7. In English, the *costumbristas* would be called writers of local color.

8. Tamayo's moral theater has a monotony similar to that of the thirteenth-century *mester de clerecía*. Whereas the thirteenth-century poet, Gonzalo de Berceo, kept writing about "the miracles of Our Lady" in monorhyme, Tamayo keeps writing about the joy of the old virtues and the wickedness of money in a kind of dramatic monorhyme. That is to say, all of his moral plays have the same sound, and their outcome, as in Berceo's "miracles," is predictable. If there is any aesthetic worth to be found in the moral plays, it is to be found in this oneness or monotony.

Twentieth-century criticism has taken kindly to the poetry of Berceo, but it has yet to take a friendly look at the moral plays of Tamayo. To use a word from England, it would dismiss Tamayo as being impossibly Victorian.

9. See D. L. Shaw, "The Anti-Romantic Reaction in Spain," *Modern Language Review,* LXIII (1968), 606-11, and also the commentary on Shaw's article in the bibliography below.

10. Galdós uses a similar metaphor in Act III of *Electra* (1901), where he likens the fusion of a man and woman in matrimony to the fusion or amalgamation of two metals in a laboratory. Even Galdós, the greatest artist of his day, could delight in such imagery!

11. Alejandro Pidal y Mon quotes Tannenberg at length in his prologue to the Fax edition of the *Complete Works,* p. 18.

12. As a young journalist, Alarcón waged an anticlerical campaign in a paper called *The Whip.* As a result of this, he fought a duel

with Heriberto García de Quevedo, who spared his life by firing his pistol into the air. Alarcón was profoundly moved by this act, and he became a convert to Catholicism.

13. According to R. Esquer Torres, it is doubtful whether or not Tamayo ever fought in a duel, although some people claimed he had said: "The author of this work has fought several times and is not about to let himself be slapped by anyone." See Esquer Torres, *El teatro de Tamayo,* p. 173.

14. See José Echegaray, *Recuerdos,* I (Madrid, 1917), 292-303. Echegaray says he wrote his memoirs "thirty or forty years" after the event, without ever seeing the play again or reading it. He forgets the names of the characters but remembers those of the actors. He remembers the broad outline of the plot and certain specific details. . . . His memoirs, which capture the essence of the play, make delightful reading.

15. Echegaray, writing from memory, did not remember the exact number of acts. The play has three acts.

16. Echegaray's memory served him well. One of the actors was called José Díez.

17. First Echegaray talks of ups and downs, and applause and protest; and then he mentions a continuous triumph. Apparently he means that the entire audience was vitally interested in the drama until the closing lines, when the words of Teodora Lamadrid made part of the audience reject it, absolutely.

18. There is some disagreement among the critics about *Duels of Honor.* For example, Esquer Torres says that at first "the work was favorably accepted by the audience as well as the critics in general, although there was some negative criticism." He goes on to say that severe criticism arose later, in 1870, when people lumped *Duels of Honor* together with *The Upright Men.* See R. Esquer Torres, *El teatro de Tamayo,* p. 172.

19. Echegaray finishes his commentary by saying that the Madrid audience was unfair to Tamayo. And then he asks, some forty years after he saw the opening performance: "Why shouldn't it [*Duels of Honor*] be shown today?" Apparently the men of the twentieth century were not interested in this kind of play.

20. There are several other interesting things in this play: the pun based on *autonomía-autonosuya*; some phrases of Paulino— "Tu reloj atrasa por lo menos un siglo"; "No empieces a diosear" (phrases that might be directed to Tamayo himself); the theme of *menosprecio de corte*; and the good dialogue.

21. See Charles B. Qualia, "The *Raisonneur* in the Social Drama

of Spain from Tamayo to Linares Rivas," *Hispania*, XIX (1936), 407-14.

22. The perfect wife, *la perfecta casada*, is one of the classic themes of Spanish literature. Fray Luis de León wrote a famous book called *La perfecta casada* in the sixteenth century.

23. To me, this speech of Fabián is rather vexing. The first ten lines or so are acceptable in the theater because a man like Don Fabián (or Tamayo) might have said them, given a challenge to a duel. But the last few lines seem stilted beyond theatrical repair. On the other hand, I have shown this text to a friend and he says: "To me they are all part of Tamayo."

24. The *raisonneur*'s was an important role and in 1862 it was played by the famous actor, Joaquín Arjona.

25. Histories and encyclopedias of Spanish literature might well refer to Tamayo as *The Raisonneur*. His name is synonymous with this dramatic figure.

26. The "scorn of court and praise of village" is another classic theme of Spanish literature. Fray Antonio de Guevara published a famous book by that name, *Menosprecio de corte y alabanza de aldea*, in 1539.

27. As I understand him, Thomas Aquinas places a great deal of emphasis on nature, and he has the supernatural order redeem it or elevate it, but not destroy it. If this is so, Tamayo's attitude is extremely un-Thomistic.

28. The Spanish text says *flor*, flower, not *rosa*, rose, but *flower* and *bread* make a most unhappy pun in English and I have used the word "rose." I think it is significant that Tamayo uses the generic term "flower," which has no color or aroma, rather than the specific term "rose," which is red and aromatic and may suggest a woman's lips or other carnal attractions. Tamayo always tends toward the abstract; indeed, he abstracts ideas from nature; he never portrays nature as she meets the eye.

29. For an explanation of *admiratio*, see E. C. Riley, *Cervantes's Theory of the Novel* (Oxford, 1962), pp. 88-94.

30. Undoubtedly, there are in our day other sources of wonderment that will seem banal a hundred years from now.

31. See Henri Bergson, *Laughter*, Doubleday Anchor Book (New York, 1956), pp. 66-67.

32. "To produce the whole of its effect, then, the comic demands something like a momentary anesthesia of the heart. Its appeal is to intelligence, pure and simple." Bergson, *op. cit.*, pp. 63-64.

33. Renan published his *Life of Jesus* in 1863, a date that corresponds to the appearance of Tamayo's moral plays (1862-1870).

I believe this chronological correspondence is important, for such a momentous work must have added fuel to the fires of Tamayo's indignation.

34. Jerónimo de Ripalda wrote a catechism of Christian doctrine and published it in Burgos in 1591. By 1900 there had been 471 editions of this book. See the monograph of J. M. Sánchez, *Doctrina cristiana del P. J. de Ripalda, e intento bibliográfico de la misma, años 1591-1900* (Madrid, 1909), as cited in the *Enciclopedia Universal Ilustrada*, Espasa-Calpe (Madrid, no date), Tomo 18, 2a. Parte, 1721.

35. One may profitably read the novels of Benito Pérez Galdós, *España sin rey* (*Spain Without a King*) and *España trágica* (*Tragic Spain*), which are part of his *Episodios nacionales*.

36. Tamayo has a theme running through this play, namely, "indignation," by which he means just wrath. The upright men are bad because they do not get angry when they ought to. The theme, however, gets swallowed up in the rhetoric of the *raisonneur*.

37. Here again there comes to mind Longfellow's translation of Jorge Manrique:

> Behold of what delusive worth
> The bubbles we pursue on earth,
> The shapes we chase,
> Amid a world of treachery!
> They vanish ere death shuts the eye,
> And leave no trace.

Tamayo's moral dramas boil down to a theatrical representation of these couplets of Jorge Manrique.

38. Free will (*libre albedrío*) had been one of the major themes of Golden Age dramatic literature.

39. Recently I saw the play Abraham Lincoln was watching the night he was assassinated, *Our American Cousin*. It bears some resemblance to Tamayo's dramas: a man of evil turns to goodness at the end and the villain is foiled by the innocent American who gives his inheritance to a humble maid. In the 1860's, virtue was still triumphant. It is interesting to note that *Our American Cousin's* evil man had turned to drink. Alcohol makes no appearance in Tamayo's plays.

40. It is difficult to overemphasize the importance of this letter as a key to Tamayo's psychology. The reader will find it in Appendix 1 of this book.

41. For a discussion of Tamayo's *alta comedia*, its attributes and its influence, see F. Ruiz Ramón, *Historia del teatro español* (Madrid, 1967), pp. 444-52; and also W. F. Smith, "Contributions of Rodríguez Rubí to the Development of the *Alta Comedia*," *Hispanic Review*, X

(1942), 53-63. A critic of the same beliefs as Tamayo was Narciso Sicars y Salvadó, who in 1906 published a long encomiastic study. He says that Tamayo's *Lo positivo* and López de Ayala's *El tanto por ciento* created "the drama of contemporary customs or *alta comedia* in which there are so happily combined the most moderate and acceptable of Romantic audacities with the polish and correction of Classicism, what is profoundly Spanish in character with the exigencies of the modern era." Sicars' statement will serve as a definition of the *alta comedia*: it is "the drama of contemporary upper middle-class customs that is moderately audacious, acceptable, correct, Spanish, and modern." See N. Sicars y Salvadó, *D. Manuel Tamayo y Baus* (Barcelona, 1906), p. 31.

42. In the case of Tamayo, it is more accurate to say language that is more or less sober, since his direful epithets hardly show more restraint than the exuberant language of Romantic playwrights.

43. Don Álvaro is the principal character of the Duke of Rivas' famous play, *La fuerza del sino* (*The Power of Fate*), 1835.

44. See Jaime Vicens Vives, *Manual de historia económica de España,* 3a. ed. (Barcelona, 1964), p. 608. I have taken my economic argument from this book and from Raymond Carr's *Spain. 1808-1939* (Oxford, 1966), Chapter VII.

45. See Carr, p. 277.

46. *Ibid.,* p. 207. See also Francisco Navarro Villoslada's novel, *La historia de muchos Pepes,* where the newspaper is the instrument of picaroons.

47. Carr's expression "rack-renter" brings to mind Maria Edgeworth's famous novel, *Castle Rackrent.* Conditions in Spain were similar in many ways to those of Ireland. See also Galdós' four *Torquemada* novels.

48. As quoted in the article on Pi y Margall, in the *Enciclopedia Universal Ilustrada,* Tomo 44 (Madrid, 1958), 406.

49. The novelist Benito Pérez Galdós found "the fitting symbol of the age" in Salamanca's genius as a speculator. See Carr, *op. cit.,* p. 281.

50. He gathered this library through the services of the well-known author, Serafín Estébanez Calderón.

51. See the Conde de Romanones, *Salamanca, conquistador de riqueza* (Madrid, 1931), p. 68.

52. After finishing my manuscript, I have come across A. A. Sicroff's article, "Américo Castro and His Critics: Eugenio Asensio," in *Hispanic Review,* XL (1972), 1-30. Perhaps Sicroff's phrase *sub specie religionis* is more accurate than the phrase I have used in this chapter, *sub specie aeternitatis.* It includes Castro's idea that

in Spain *la vida religiosa asfixiaba la vida secular—una vida secular que nadie concibió en España como válida en sí misma* (p. 23). Sicroff sees Castro's opinion as a key to "the organic meaning for a variety of aspects of Spanish life." I should add that it is a key to various aspects of Tamayo's life.

Chapter Three

1. In the present study I have accepted Webster's definition of melodrama: "an extravagantly theatrical play in which action and plot predominate over characterization." (See *Webster's Seventh New Collegiate Dictionary.*) Tamayo's *Ángela*, which is treated in the present chapter, conforms perfectly to the definition. Although Tamayo's humorous pieces are not melodramas, they do subordinate characterization to action and plot; thus they may be grouped with *Ángela* as entertainments.

2. Chapter 4 will study the three historical dramas and the tragedy *Virginia*, which is also historical since it is based on a famous episode from Roman history. Chapter 5 is devoted to two plays about jealousy, *La bola de nieve* and *Un drama nuevo*, which posterity has accepted as Tamayo's masterpiece. Chapters 3, 4, and 5 do not exhaust Tamayo's theater since they do not include many plays he wrote as a young man. Consequently Chapter 6 will study those early plays not studied elsewhere in this book. Chapter 7 will examine Tamayo's discourse on aesthetics, "Truth, the Source of Beauty in Dramatic Literature"; it will also state a *Conclusion*.

3. See Neale H. Tayler, *Las fuentes del teatro de Tamayo y Baus* (Madrid, 1959), pp. 117-21.

4. See Tayler, pp. 128-32.

5. A Greene novel, on the other hand, has a theological meaning. It may or may not have a fascinating plot intended mostly to entertain, but it must communicate a higher truth. Examples of Greene's novels are *The Power and the Glory* and *The Heart of the Matter*. Examples of his entertainments are *The Ministry of Fear* and *This Gun for Hire*.

6. Tamayo the moralist peeps out from behind the curtains at the end of *Ángela*. San Mario repents his evil deeds and invokes God's mercy. The mood is again Jorge Manrique's "This world is the rugged road that leads to the next world." This episode is so brief it does not destroy the entertainment, although it does show poor judgment on Tamayo's part. A modern screenwriter would surely eliminate it.

7. Tamayo goes on to specify what he has imitated, e.g., "the final scene of the second act and the scene of San Mario and Angela in the third." For a comparative study of Tamayo and Schiller, see

Egon Schwarz, "Manuel Tamayo y Baus and Schiller," in *Comparative Literature*, XIII (1961), 123-37.

8. See Calvin Thomas, *The Life and Works of Friedrich Schiller* (Holt: New York, 1901), p. 132.

9. See *Love and Intrigue*, English version by Friedrich Rolf, Barron's Educational Series (Great Neck, New York, 1962), p. 10 (Act I, Scene i).

10. Thomas, *op cit.*, p. 134; and Thomas Carlyle, *The Life of Friedrich Schiller* (London: Taylor and Hessey, 1825), p. 57.

11. The Spanish playwright, José Echegaray, says in his *Memoirs* that he attended the opening performance of Tamayo's *Ángela*. Not only were there shouts and cries of *bravo*, "but many of the spectators threw their hats on the stage." Echegaray reasons that Tamayo has the knack of materializing a conflict, of making it visible to the audience so that the latter will applaud it. See José Echegaray, *Recuerdos*, I (Madrid, 1917), 29-32.

Chapter Four

1. *OC*, 244.

2. The full title of Juan de la Cueva's play is *La muerte de Virginia*. See *OC*, 253-54. The letter to Manuel Cañete, which appears in *OC*, 244-47, was published as a prologue to Tamayo's *Virginia*.

3. I am using Tamayo's Spanish orthography rather than the Latin orthography, e.g., Virginio instead of Virginius, Icilio instead of Icilius, and so forth.

4. There were two creative decades in Tamayo's life, during which his plays appeared: 1847-1856 and 1862-1870. During the first decade he wrote half his plays in verse and the other half in prose. During the second decade he wrote everything in prose. The question of Tamayo's use of verse is discussed below, in Chapter 5, under *La bola de nieve*.

5. I showed this passage of my manuscript to a fellow Hispanist, who suggested: "Or maybe it was Tamayo's deference to the *paterfamilias* idea of the Romans, the respect for the head of the family." Be that as it may, Tamayo's motive is not so important as the effect Icilio's conduct has on the play. Again, let it be said that Icilio acts like a puppet.

6. For another dramatic use of *luto*, mourning, see the plays of Federico García Lorca, *Blood Wedding* and *The House Of Bernarda Alba*. If properly used by the director of a play, *luto* provides a very telling spectacle in the Spanish theater.

7. See the 1947 Fax edition of the *OC*, 244-57. Cañete's reply to Tamayo appears on pages 257-61.

8. He singles out for special mention the *Edipo* (*Oedipus*) of Martínez de la Rosa, the *Pelayo* of Quintana, and the *Sara* of Cervino.

9. There are many preceptists, Tamayo says, who would rather see the demise of tragedy than see it reborn under a new form, adequate to the contemporary scene; as if there could be only one tragedy, the classic tragedy, the Greek. Tamayo writes: "But would it not be a salutary lesson to make visible on the stage the extreme anguish and degradation of an impulsive man who is excited by a disordered passion?" Tamayo is always conscious of exemplarity, of teaching a lesson.

10. Medea does these things without any inner debate, that is, without the variety of thoughts, passions, and feelings that attend an inner struggle. Tamayo seems to be echoing here Lope de Vega's idea in *The New Art of Writing Dramas* (1609), namely, that in nature variety is the source of beauty.

11. As symbols of modern agitation, Tamayo mentions the steamboat, the locomotive, and the fact that "the human word crosses space on the wings of thought." Since he was writing in 1853, I construe the last statement to mean the semaphore rather than the wireless.

12. The "dearest friend" is Manuel Cañete (1822-1891), to whom the letter is addressed.

13. See Prof. J. Alberich's book review of *La poética de Campoamor* in the *Bulletin of Hispanic Studies*, XLVII (1970), 265: ". . . the nineteenth century is filled with men who think well and write badly. The same study could have been made of Lista, an excellent critic and author of mediocre verses, or of Tamayo, whose most discerning ideas on the theater did not prevent him from writing frightful melodramas."

14. See, for example, Leopoldo Augusto de Cueto, *Estudios de historia y de crítica literaria* (Madrid, 1900), pp. 391-436, where the author discusses the Roman legend of Virginia in dramatic literature.

15. In 1841, Tamayo staged a play called *Genoveva de Brabante*, in which his mother played the leading role. He was eleven years old at the time, and the audience was visibly moved when, at the curtain call, the author came forth with his mother. (See the speech of Aureliano Fernández-Guerra y Orbe, "Discurso de contestación," in *Discursos leídos en las recepciones públicas qua ha celebrado desde 1847 la Real Academia Española*, Tomo Segundo [Madrid, 1860], 293-94.) Critics have never uncovered a copy of this play, and so it constitutes a pious anecdote in a study of the present kind. *Juana de Arco* must be considered his first play.

16. See James Westfall Thompson, *An Introduction to Medieval Europe* (New York, 1937), p. 890.

17. Concerning Voltaire, see Calvin Thomas, *The Life and Works of Friedrich Schiller* (New York, 1901), p. 382.

18. Schiller's drama has an Augustinian grandeur. It concerns the earthly city and the city of God, and Joan, the maiden who held citizenship in both of them. Schiller seems to be saying that the earthly city cannot exist by itself; it is the scene of strife and civil war until the invisible city, the City of God, sends a messenger. When this messenger comes and soothes the discord in men's breasts, the earthly city will have love and fraternity. But the messenger must be sacrificed. Tamayo's drama, written when he was eighteen years old, has no such grandeur. It merely tells the story of Joan.

19. *The Works of Friedrich Schiller*, III (London, 1854), 437.

20. *Ibid.*, 442.

21. In other words, Tamayo has taken Schiller's great drama, retold its action, and stripped it of its profound meaning. He sticks to what Schiller called "the sensible" (the palpable) and ignores the Schillerian "ideal."

22. Even the historical drama, *La locura de amor,* has its counterpart in a play like Hugo's *Hernani,* whereas *La ricahembra* is uniquely Spanish.

23. See R. Esquer Torres, *El teatro de Tamayo y Baus,* pp. 78-79. See also Tamayo, *OC,* 565.

24. A major difference between Tamayo's *Doña Juana* and the typical Spanish seventeenth-century *comedia* as established by Lope de Vega is the number of acts; Tamayo has four whereas Lope fixed the Spanish norm as three. What Tamayo has done, in effect, is to write a three-act Lopesque *comedia,* with a one-act prologue, the prologue consisting of the face slapping and marriage, and the *comedia* proper of the enamored secretary who writes *Doña Juana* a love letter.

25. It is uncanny how two men like Tamayo and Ramón del Valle-Inclán (1866-1936) are instinctive opposites. Valle's *sonata, Cuento de abril,* written seventy years after *La ricahembra,* praises the courtly love of Provence and makes light of the love I have called Castilian. It would appear that all men, even Spanish *modernistas,* are rigorously logical; if two authors start out at opposite theological poles, they will end up opposites in almost everything they write.

26. These lines refer to the Battle of Aljubarrota, in 1385. The action of the play takes place in 1386. Juan I was king from 1379 to 1390. G. Hubbard (see the Bibliography) mistakenly places the action of the play in the reign of Peter the Cruel, who reigned from

1350 to 1369. See also the criticism of P. Francisco Blanco García, whose name appears in the Bibliography.

27. At the end of *La ricahembra,* Tamayo writes an interesting note about the face-slapping incident: "Even between two men, our audience today does not tolerate the representation on the stage of such a terrible outrage. The art of the actor who plays the role of Don Alonso consists, then, in showing that he stretches out to close the mouth of Doña Juana so that she cannot go on; although he must give to this gesture all the rudeness and violence that are necessary to justify the resolution (the most unusual marriage) of the female magnate" (*OC,* p. 566).

There are several *ripios* (padded verses) in *La ricahembra,* e.g., the verses of Act III, Scene v. This book will discuss Tamayo's use of verse under *La bola de nieve.*

28. Lest the name Doña Juana cause confusion, the reader is advised that Doña Juana the magnate (*La ricahembra*) and Doña Juana the mad queen of Castile are not one and the same person. The lady magnate lived in the fourteenth century; the mad queen, mother of the emperor Charles V, lived well into the sixteenth century.

29. See Narciso Sicars y Salvadó, *D. Manuel Tamayo y Baus* (Barcelona, 1906), pp. 253 ff. In 1969, the author of the present study saw a performance of *La locura de amor* in Mexico City, where it was well received. The play has also been made into a well-known Spanish movie.

30. See R. R. Ashburn's edition of Tamayo's *La locura de amor* (New York, 1931), p. xxi.

31. *Ibid.,* p. xxii.

Chapter Five

1. A *romance* is a verse form that repeats the same assonance at the end of all even-numbered lines and does not give the odd-numbered lines any rhyme at all. The Spanish ballads consist of octosyllabic verses rhyming in assonance. A *redondilla* is a verse form consisting of four octosyllabic verses, of which the first rhymes with the last and the second with the third. See Hymen Alpern and José Martel, *Diez comedias del siglo de oro* (Harper: New York, 1939), pp. xxv-xxviii.

2. A *décima* consists of ten octosyllabic verses of which, generally speaking, the first rhymes with the fourth and fifth, the second with the third, the sixth with the seventh, and the last with the eighth and ninth. See Alpern and Martel, *loc. cit.*

3. A *quintilla* consists of five octosyllabic verses, which have

two different consonant rhymes. These are generally arranged in such a way that three straight lines do not rhyme, nor do the fourth and fifth. See Alpern and Martel, *loc. cit.*

4. As suggested by Alpern and Martel, p. xxvii.

5. The act and verse numbers of *Slave of the Devil, No One Beneath the King* and *Treat Disdain with Disdain* are taken from Alpern and Martel, *op. cit.*

6. In May, 1856, Don Juan Valera wrote a long article defending Tamayo against his critics. According to Valera, *The Snowball* was well staged and generally well received; however, some people, he says, "go to the theater looking for a certain philosophy or morality, and if they don't find it they criticize the author bitterly." Thus Tamayo (according to Valera) was attacked by his enemies; but the accusations against him are false. See Valera, *Obras completas,* II (Madrid, 1942), 56-61.

7. Past criticism has often referred to *The Snowball* as one of the plays of the *alta comedia.* This to me is in error; I have studied it separately because it is not concerned with the evils of money or the evils of modern industry and politics; in a word, with the alleged evils of the upper middle class. Its theme is jealousy.

8. See Charles David Ley, *El gracioso en el teatro de la península* (Madrid, 1954), pp. 46, 53, 204-25. In the third act, Tamayo's Juana tries to acquire dignity. This effort is sudden and lacks verisimilitude.

9. For orphans, see for example, Charles Dickens, *Oliver Twist,* and José María Pereda, *Sotileza.* For misers, see Balzac, *Eugénie Grandet,* George Eliot, *Silas Marner,* and Benito Pérez Galdós, the four *Torquemada* novels.

10. Tamayo's aesthetics are the subject of Chapter 7, which explains his doctrine of forms.

11. The Spanish title of this play, which will be examined in Chapter 6, is *Hija y Madre.*

12. It is interesting to go over the cast of characters in Tamayo's plays and those who took the roles. From 1852 on, the most famous actors of Madrid were taking the parts he created. Doña Teodora Lamadrid played the roles of Ángela, Virginia, Doña Juana the magnate, the Queen Doña Juana, the Countess, and Clara, the jealous woman of *La bola de nieve.* Don Joaquín Arjona took the roles of the Prince San Mario, Virginio, Beltrán, King Philip, old Andrés, and Fernando, the young gentleman of *La bola de nieve.* Tamayo's brother Victorino, an outstanding actor of the day, also acted in all his plays. In other words, the actors as well as the audiences were applauding Tamayo.

13. P. Francisco Blanco García, *La literatura española en el siglo XIX,* 3a. edición (Madrid, 1910), p. 174.

14. Angel del Río, *Historia de la literatura española,* Edición revisada, II (New York, 1963), 171.

15. In Tamayo's drama, Yorick is not the buffoon of *Hamlet,* but a contemporary of Shakespeare, a comic actor now turned tragic.

16. The resemblance to Hippolytus and Phaedre is obvious. Edmundo, however, is less innocent than Hippolytus, and Alicia is not nearly so culpable as Phaedre. A closer likeness may be seen in Lope de Vega's *Castigo sin venganza.*

17. The following diagram may help the reader to understand the action:

Tamayo's play (which becomes "real life")	The play-within-the-play (which becomes "the theater")
Yorick, an outraged husband, plays the part of ...	Count Octavio, an outraged husband
Alicia, Yorick's young wife, in love with his son, plays the part of	Beatriz, Octavio's young wife, in love with his son
Edmundo, Yorick's son, in love with his father's wife, plays the part of	Manfredo, Octavio's son, in love with his father's wife
Walton, Yorick's enemy, plays the part of...........	Landolfo, Octavio's enemy

18. Remember, they are part of Shakespeare's company.

19. Past comparative studies have likened *A New Drama* to Lope de Vega's *Lo fingido verdadero,* Kyd's *The Spanish Tragedy,* Shakespeare's *Hamlet* and *Othello,* Rotrou's *Saint Genest* and Dumas Père's *Kean ou Désordre et Génie,* but they have not pointed out its likeness to Lope's *El castigo sin venganza.* Both plays are rather like a *Phèdre* in which Hippolytus is not entirely innocent. Lope's Duke has Federico unwittingly execute Casandra, without vengeance (*sin venganza*), whereas Tamayo's Yorick executes Edmundo in the presence of Alicia, and with vengeance (*con venganza*). Thus *Un drama nuevo* might also be titled *El castigo con venganza.*

One of Yorick's speeches in Act I, Scene iii is especially reminiscent of Lope. Yorick thinks Edmundo is distant toward him from envy of Alicia, who has taken first place in his own affections; similarly, in Lope's play, the Duke fears that Federico will envy Casandra, his new bride, for displacing him in the Duke's affections.

20. These forms will be discussed in Chapter 7, which concerns Tamayo's aesthetics.

21. Tirso de Molina's Paulo in *El condenado por desconfiado* may seem similar to Edmundo on the question of salvation, but his sin is much more profound. He is the opposite of the Don Juan of Tirso's *Burlador de Sevilla*, whose specific sin is presumption; Paulo's sin is despair. Both men offend the theological virtue of hope.

22. This is not to say that Tamayo suddenly read Lope's disquisition and carefully and consciously followed it. It means rather that *Un drama nuevo* immediately brings Lope's ideas to mind, so much so that Tamayo must have been following that great master's example, consciously or unconsciously. Thus, an examination of Lope's *New Art of Writing Dramas* will throw light on Tamayo's *Un drama nuevo*.

23. The source says "four editions," but apparently means "printings." See J. D. Fitz-Gerald, "*Un Drama Nuevo* on the American Stage," *Hispania*, VII (1924), 171.

24. See Lester G. Crocker, "Techniques Of Ambiguity in *Un Drama Nuevo*," *Hispania*, XXXIX (1956), 412-18.

25. *El arte nuevo de hacer comedias* consists of 396 verses, directed to the Academy of Madrid in 1609. In speaking of variety, Lope is referring to the mixture of tragedy and comedy, which can also be seen in Tamayo's tragicomedy, *Un drama nuevo*. I have taken some liberty with the word "variety."

I should add that there is no figure of fun (*gracioso*) in *Un drama nuevo*. Tamayo was an extremely serious man, apparently incapable of bringing a clown into a play about jealousy. One critic has spoken of "the scrupulous and brooding nineteenth century." See Roy Temple House, "Lope de Vega and *Un drama nuevo*," *Romanic Review*, XIII (1922), 86.

Chapter Six

1. Blanche Emma Goodell lists fifty plays, Ramón Esquer Torres, thirty-five. See Goodell, "Manuel Tamayo y Baus," unpublished University of Wisconsin Doctoral Dissertation, Madison, 1950, pp. 242-44; and Esquer Torres, *El teatro de Tamayo y Baus* (Madrid, 1965), the *Indice*.

2. The Fax edition presents the two versions Tamayo wrote of *Virginia*, but I count them as one play.

3. This short definition of the *loa* adequately describes Tamayo's verses, although it does not take in all *loas*. For a more lengthy discussion of the *loa*, in English, see Gerard Flynn, *Sor Juana Inés de la Cruz* (New York: Twayne Publishers, 1971), *passim*.

4. This *loa* makes such a strong condemnation of civil war that it appears to be anti-Carlist in sentiment. Elsewhere, however, Tamayo declares he is a Carlist. See Chapter 1 and Appendix 1 of the present study.

5. See R. Esquer Torres, *El teatro de Tamayo y Baus,* pp. 21-22.

6. A year later, in 1852, Tamayo wrote another *loa* to the Princess of Asturias.

7. In the Spanish Golden Age, many authors converted profane works into religious ones. An example is Fray Bartolomé Ponce's *Clara Diana a lo divino* (1582), which was based on Montemayor's pastoral novel *La Diana* (*ca.* 1559). Tamayo saw everything in a divine light. He did not write Romantic plays, he merely used Romantic garments to clothe a Christian message.

8. The anagnorisis in *El cinco de agosto* and *El castillo de Balsaín* also resembles Cervantes' *Novelas ejemplares* and the novels of chivalry. See *La Gitanilla, La ilustre fregona;* also *Don Quijote* (1605), Ch. XXI: *porque se vino a averiguar que·el tal caballero es hijo de un valeroso rey.* In Ch. XXI, Don Quijote describes the plot of a model novel of chivalry.

9. See D. L. Shaw, "Towards the Understanding of Spanish Romanticism," *Modern Language Review,* LXIII (1968), 606-11.

10. Tamayo's Romantic vocabulary is so excessive at times that it calls to mind Ramón de Mesonero Romanos' (1803-1882) famous article, "El romanticismo y los románticos," from the *Escenas matritenses.*

11. See Neale Tayler, *Las fuentes del teatro de Tamayo y Baus,* pp. 115-17.

12. *Tran-Tran,* a musical farce, is a *zarzuela; Don Simplicio Bobadilla,* a musical spectacle, is a *zarzuela.* E. B. Williams' *Diccionario del idioma español* defines the term as "a Spanish theatrical work in which declamation and song are alternated." It should be noted that *Don Simplicio Bobadilla* is an imitation of the famous magic play (*comedia de magia*), *Pata de Cabra,* which also has a character called Don Simplicio. It first appeared in 1828.

13. Don Simplicio's full name is Simplicio Bobadilla de Majaderano y Cabeza de Buey. Because of its likeness to the Spanish words *simple* and *bobada* the name Simplicio Bobadilla may be translated as Foolery Humbug, a phrase that describes the action of the play. *Majaderano* resembles *majadero,* silly, and Cabeza de Buey, Oxhead, is apparently a play on the name of the Spanish *conquistador,* Alvar Núñez Cabeza da Vaca. Although Bobadilla is the surname of a famous contemporary of Columbus, Simplicio Bobadilla is a dumb ox.

14. There is a memorable *cuento ruso* (Russian story) about a snow child the sun melted in Africa (Act II, Scene ii) and a passage resembling the talking-animal dialogues in Pío Baroja's *Paradox, rey* (1906).

Chapter Seven

1. *Discurso leído ante la Real Academia Española por Manuel Tamayo y Baus, en su recepción pública, el día 12 de junio de 1859,* in his *Obras completas* (Madrid: Fax, 1947), pp. 1133-64.

2. Tamayo was only twenty-eight years old when he was elected to the Academy, and twenty-nine when he read his acceptance speech. The reader might compare his age on entrance into the Academy with the ages of other famous authors who became academicians. Manuel Bretón de los Herreros was forty-four on his entrance; José Zorrilla, sixty-five; Juan Valera, thirty-seven; Pedro Antonio de Alarcón, forty-four; José María de Pereda, sixty-three; Benito Pérez Galdós, fifty-four (Galdós was elected at the age of forty-six, but he deferred reading his speech.) The only nineteenth-century author to enter the Academy at a younger age than Tamayo was Marcelino Menéndez Pelayo, at twenty-five. But he did so (in 1881) long after Tamayo, so that Tamayo's selection must have seemed truly unusual.

3. The first two parts of Tamayo's speech take up some 330 words.

4. Tamayo's attitude stands in contrast to that of many members, e.g., Benito Pérez Galdós (1843-1920) and José Zorrilla (1817-1893). Galdós delayed eight years before reading his acceptance speech and finally did so only at the urging of Pereda and others; see H. Chonon Berkowitz, *Pérez Galdós* (Madison, 1948), pp. 226-35. Zorrilla wanted to put one of his tales (*leyendas*) into verse and read that as an acceptance speech; see the *Boletín de la Real Academia,* Tomo 39 (1959), 96.

5. By "moral" Tamayo means any thought, word, or deed that is specifically human. Thus, the contemplation of the meaning of happiness, or the value of money, is a moral act; it is the very stuff that theater is made of.

6. I say "near-synonym" because sometimes Tamayo uses "reality," "nature," and "truth" interchangeably, whereas at other times he does not; again he is apt to use "truth" as the conformation of the mind, or the character in a play, to reality. As we shall see below, Tamayo also uses the word *forma* in two distinct ways, and this is likely to cause serious confusion. A professional philosopher would be sure to use a more precise vocabulary.

7. In Tamayo's system, the birth of a work of art, like the birth of a child, is a procreation. It is the marvelous production (repro-

duction) of something new by a finite creature. Since the author is not infinite, or ultimate, his work is not a creation, but an extension of creation, a procreation.

8. Tamayo's speech is not as syllogistic in appearance as my paragraph may suggest. Nevertheless, it is syllogistic in the sense that Tamayo is a man who offers premises from which certain conclusions must follow. His Major Premise is God: "He is the only creator." Since many twentieth-century critics reject Tamayo's premises, they quite logically, in the eyes of a man like Tamayo, reject his theater.

9. Tamayo would say "reproduce," not "produce," "represent," not "present"; the re- suggests secondary causation.

10. "Sensible" means: (a) capable of being perceived by the senses, and (b) perceptible to the mind. I construe the word to have both meanings in Tamayo's essay. It follows that (a) The theater will make use of anything appealing to the senses to get a form across to the spectator; thus colors, music, gestures, objects, in a word, the palpable, will be used to get across, for example, the gratitude of a son or daughter; (b) This Tamayesque form, gratitude, is "sensible" because it inheres somehow in matter. The form itself is immaterial, it proceeds from the soul, but it is "sensible" when it is apprehended by the mind. This question of the "sensible" is important because Tamayo excludes some things from the theater which he considers to be nonsensible. They cannot properly be called forms because they pertain to the *great beyond*; an example of this is the paternal love of the Almighty or an absolute idea of the beautiful, the true, and the good. *Pero este infinito* más allá *concebido por una esencia infinita, no es sino presentimiento y esperanza, tipo espiritual extraño a forma alguna, idea pura, en fin, incapaz de convertirse en imagen sensible* (*OC*, 1135).

11. Thus art is a kind of revelation, the revelation of forms. Tamayo also speaks of *deleitar aprovechando* (*OC*, 1142): "to cause delight giving profit," which is like Horace's *dulce et utile*. This was the goal of art in Cervantes and the Golden Age authors; see E. C. Riley, *Cervantes's Theory of the Novel* (Oxford: Clarendon Press, 1962), pp. 81-87. Thus Tamayo explicitly identifies himself with Cervantes and the men of his era.

12. Pagan Greece furnishes a good example of Tamayo's doctrine that the ugly is representable in art provided it is not treated as an end in itself. *Oedipus Rex* faithfully reproduces (re-presents) the ugly as it appeared in Greece, and when we see Oedipus striving to comprehend it, though he cannot, when we see him "impetuously

rising up" as his children are taken from him, we know that the ugly is not something desirable, that is, it is not an acceptable end.

13. The greatest dramatists of seventeenth-century Spain, Lope de Vega, Tirso de Molina, and Pedro Calderón de la Barca were ordained priests.

14. In Tamayo's vision, then, the playwrights of Elizabethan England and Golden Age Spain were "romantics." Since the characters of their theater have free will, the form of their theater is not restrained by the classical unities. Their theater is free and varied, as human life is free and varied, and this correspondence of theater to life is what Tamayo means by "romantic."

15. The question of form is apt to cause confusion, since Tamayo uses the word in two different ways without spelling out their difference. In Tamayo's essay there is a metaphysical form and an artistic form. They will be discussed below, in the section called *A Critique of Tamayo's Aesthetics.*

16. By "general rule," Tamayo means that nature shuns the unusual or extreme. This holds for the good as well as evil. An author should not put an ideal saint in his plays, a sort of pure spirit who never has to contend with obstacles. Neither should he put an incarnate devil on the stage, a man who is never attracted to the good. By nature's not concentrating on evil, Tamayo means that evil cannot be an end in itself. If there is a drama in which suicide is portrayed as a satisfactory solution to human life, or in which an evil man, a God-defier, is portrayed as heroic, then that drama is false; and being false, not true, it is not beautiful. In spite of its correct form, which is romantic, it is not good art because it has made the ugly into an end.

17. In a chapter on "Imitation and Creation," Hazard Adams uses the words "content" and "container." See *The Interests of Criticism, an Introduction to Literary Theory* (New York, 1969), p. 18.

18. Tamayo is aware of the difference between *fondo* and *forma.* Thus he writes, in his Academy speech: *Y puesto que la dramática debe ser verdadera en el fondo, cúmplele parecerlo también en la forma, lo mismo en la idea que en el signo que la exprese; juntamente en la manera de sentir y en el modo de hablar (OC, 1143).* Nevertheless, he keeps applying the word *forma,* on the one hand, to *la idea* and *la manera de sentir,* and also, on the other, to *el signo que la exprese* and *el modo de hablar;* that is, he applies the word *forma* to both the content and the container. Thus, some attempt at critical elucidation is necessary.

19. According to the dictionary of the Spanish Royal Academy, hylomorphism is the "theory conceived by Aristotle and followed by

the majority of the Scholastics, according to which every body is
constituted of two essential principles, which are matter and form."
It is important to note that in his Academy speech Tamayo does
not mention Aristotle or any other philosopher, nor does he refer
to a given philosophy.

20. Tamayo obviously departs here from Aristotle, for whom
evil is a *privatio boni*, a kind of nothingness. Tamayo is apparently
speaking with poetic license.

21. As we saw above, Tamayo uses the terms "the true," "the
real," and "nature" interchangeably. Thus in him the definition of
nature is the true and the real, both in objects and subjects, externally
and internally. By "the true and the real" he seems to mean what-
ever exists in the world, physically and metaphysically.

22. In Aristotle, what Tamayo calls the "invisible essence" would
be the form, or soul, and a virtue such as gratitude would be a
habit of the soul. But Tamayo calls the virtues and other habits
formas, and he calls the soul the "invisible essence."

23. From a philosophical point of view, the question of evil presents a grave problem here. It is unthinkable that Tamayo would
attribute evil to God; nevertheless, in his doctrine of forms, he
seems to give it a kind of existence. Perhaps one can argue that a
manifestation of the soul, such as hate or murderous action, is a
mis-direction, a turning away from existence, and so not attributable
to the Creator. Or again, one can argue that Tamayo speaks with
"poetic license." In any case, he does not think through the problem
of evil as it applies to his theory of forms.

24. Tamayo can pass from the world of nonsensible forms to the
world of sensible forms, from the metaphysical world to the physical
world, from the invisible world to the visible world with comparative
ease, for to him both worlds are really one. Both worlds come from
God, who can neither deceive nor be deceived. Tamayo's aesthetics
are, above all, theological; everything, including the theater, is directed
to God. The final cause of the theater is salvation, union with God.
In the Academy speech, as seen above, he says "God is the only
creator" (*OC*, 1135); and in the prologue to *Ángela,* where he also
states his aesthetic philosophy, he writes: "The principles of my
dramatic poetics are enclosed in this sentence: 'Men, and above
men, God' " (*OC*, 154).

25. I realize that for some critics there can be no separation of
fondo and *forma.* My purpose, however, is to clarify Tamayo's
position, not to write a disquisition on modern aesthetics. I shall
merely say that for Tamayo his *Forma* I, which is ultimately the
content of God's creation, is what is most significant in art; the poet's

word must imitate it. For a twentieth-century poet like Pedro Salinas, on the other hand, the *Forma* II, the *logos* of the poet, is alone significant in art; the content does not count at all. That is why Salinas can unhesitatingly praise Valle-Inclán's *Sonatas*, which many people consider to be scandalous. See Pedro Salinas, *Literatura española siglo XX*, 2a. *edición aumentada* (México, 1948), p. 101, the passage beginning with the words *El que crea, como yo . . .*

26. After I finished typing this passage, I heard the Milwaukee Symphony Orchestra play the Prelude and Liebestod from *Tristan und Isolde*. I can see now why Tamayo considers music a formless, inferior art; for him a piece like the *Liebestod* is too uncanny. It is not susceptible of rational explanation. Tamayo's dramatic world is a planet in a larger world resembling the Ptolemaic universe, with its fixed center, where everything has a place, everything a destination. There is no room for a stammer.

A mystic like St. John of the Cross is a lyrical poet, that is to say, a musical poet. He is known for his stammer (*balbuceo*), especially the verse *un no sé qué que queda balbuciendo*. Tamayo, on the other hand, in spite of his total emphasis on religion, is the least mystical and the least musical of authors. He is a logician.

27. In the previous paragraph I have said that "characters like Clara and Luis change their minds too quickly and too often." My present statement does not contradict that opinion. Sudden changes of mind, changes that lack verisimilitude, e.g., the sudden conversion of a villain or a sudden happy ending, appear in many plays. Thus, sudden changes of mind are a constant, an invariable, in Tamayo's theater.

28. In his review of a book called *La poética de Campoamor*, J. Alberich has written the following words: "His [the author's] object was to show the originality and sureness of the aesthetic judgments of Campoamor, in contrast with the obvious crudeness of his verse. And this task . . . was worthwhile, because the Spanish nineteenth century is filled with men who think well and write badly. The same study could have been made of Lista, an excellent critic and an author of mediocre verses, or of Tamayo, whose most correct ideas concerning the theater didn't keep him from writing frightful melodramas . . ."; see the *Bulletin of Hispanic Studies*, XLVII (1970), 265. Apparently Tamayo was not the only author who failed to practice on occasion his own aesthetic doctrine.

Selected Bibliography

PRIMARY SOURCES

1. Editions of Tamayo's Works. Collections

Obras. 4 volumes (Madrid: Rivadeneyra, 1898-1900). There is a long prologue to volume I by Alejandro Pidal y Mon (1846-1913).

Obras completas de Tamayo y Baus (Madrid: Editorial Fax, 1947). Includes the 1898 prologue to the *Obras* of Alejandro Pidal y Mon. In spite of the title, *Complete Works,* this collection is not complete. It contains eighteen (this figure includes both versions of *Virginia*) of the twenty-three plays studied in the present work, and also Tamayo's Royal Academy speech.

The Oberlin College Spanish Drama Collection (862.08, SP 24, 311). Contains five of the twenty-three plays studied in the present work. Also contains plays by Tamayo's brothers, Andrés and Victorino.

2. Editions of Tamayo's Works. Single Plays

Una apuesta and *Huyendo del perejil,* edited by Cony Sturgis and Juanita C. Robinson (New York: The Macmillan Company, 1930). A students' edition with notes, exercises, and a Spanish-English vocabulary.

Un drama nuevo, edited by R. T. House and A. M. Kaufman (New York: Allyn and Bacon, 1923). A students' edition with notes, exercises, and a Spanish-English vocabulary.

Un drama nuevo, edited by Clarence King Moore and J. Horace Nunemaker. 2nd edition (New York: Silver Burdett Co., 1937). A students' edition with notes, exercises, and a Spanish-English vocabulary.

La locura de amor, edited by Robert M. Ashburn (New York: Prentice-Hall, 1931). The introduction gives a detailed account of the historical setting of *La locura de amor.* Was Doña Juana really insane? "The historians say yes, the poets say no." Gives a detailed bibliography of Tamayo's plays and of secondary authorities down to 1931. A students' edition with notes and a Spanish-English vocabulary.

Lo positivo, edited by Philip Harry and Alfonso De Salvio (New York: D. C. Heath and Co., 1908). The introduction argues that Tamayo and Adelardo López de Ayala attempted to lead the Spanish theater, which was being monopolized by the Romanticists, back to truth and common sense. A students' edition with notes and a Spanish-English vocabulary.

3. A Special Reference

The reader is also referred to the many articles by R. Esquer Torres, which appear below under *Secondary Sources*. These articles contain many letters written by Tamayo to distinguished contemporaries. As my Chapter 1 indicates, most of Tamayo's personal papers were destroyed right after his death. This was done in keeping with his will.

SECONDARY SOURCES

ALARCÓN, PEDRO ANTONIO DE. "Discurso sobre la moral en el arte," in *Obras completas* (Madrid: Ediciones Fax, 1954), pp. 1748-63. Alarcón read this speech on his entrance into the Royal Academy in 1877. Opposes the idolatry of Art-for-Art's Sake. Argues that although morality cannot be considered the exclusive criterion of artistic beauty, neither can there be artistic beauty indifferent to morality. Argues that Art is "the great conservative element." This speech throws light on Tamayo's aesthetics and on his thesis dramas.

ALAS, LEOPOLDO (pseud. "CLARÍN"). "Tamayo," in *Solos y Paliques, Obras selectas* (Madrid: Biblioteca Nueva, 1947), pp. 1013-19. Argues that Tamayo has written the most perfect drama of the nineteenth-century Spanish theater, *A New Drama*, although he is not the greatest dramatic poet of his day. Discusses his "ethical theater." Compares him with Juan Ruiz de Alarcón (seventeenth century) and Victorien Sardou (nineteenth century).

ALBERICH, JOSÉ. "El papel de Shakespeare en *Un drama nuevo de* Tamayo," Filología Moderna, X, no. 39 (1970), 301-22. Argues that Tamayo consistently and firmly sets forth his dramatic principles, e.g., in the prologue to *Virginia* and the Academy speech. Therefore it is incorrect to say, as many critics have done, that *A New Drama* is an amoral, fatalistic work. Tamayo's Shakespeare is the spokesman of his theatrical and moral ideas.

I read this article after finishing my manuscript of the present work, so I have not mentioned it elsewhere in the text. It contains many points of interest; e.g., on page 302, note 3, one learns that Tamayo's Academy speech owes a debt to Schlegel's *Course of Dramatic Literature.*

BARJA, CESAR. *Libros y autores modernos* (New York: G. E. Stechert, 1924), pp. 377-90. Argues that on the demise of Romanticism, Tamayo and Adelardo López de Ayala represent "the prudence of transition, the equilibrium of rest, and the reign of common sense." Has a low opinion of Tamayo's thesis plays. "The true Tamayo is in the dramas of pure art, namely, *Virginia, La Rica Hembra, La locura de amor, Un drama nuevo.*"

BLANCO GARCÍA, FRANCISCO. *La literatura española en el siglo XIX.* 3a. edición. Parte Segunda (Madrid: Sáenz de Jubera Hnos., 1910), pp. 159-78. A history of Spanish literature written by a contemporary of Tamayo. Argues that Tamayo is the greatest Spanish playwright of the nineteenth century. Studies his most prominent plays, one by one.

CEJADOR Y FRAUCA, JULIO. *Historia de la lengua y literatura castellana,* VIII (Madrid: Tip. de la "Revista de Archivos, Bibl. y Museos," 1918), 116-23. Argues that Tamayo was the first to take from Romanticism "the delightful new fruits of the true modern drama." Discusses his arrangements from the French, his pseudonyms, his politics after 1868, his thesis plays "seen through Christian glasses," and his theatrical silence after 1870.

COTARELO Y MORI, EMILIO. *Discursos leídos en la Real Academia Española el día 27 de octubre de 1929 para celebrar el centenario del nacimiento de Don Manuel Tamayo y Baus* (Madrid: Tipografía de Archivos, 1929). Three speeches by Emilio Cotarelo y Mori, Manuel de Sandoval, and Serafín and Joaquín Álvarez Quintero celebrating the centenary of Tamayo's birth. Cotarelo's speech has biographical information not contained in other sources. The Álvarez Quintero brothers say that Tamayo in some of his works became "a father of souls, and that he tried to save them with moral warnings and examples somewhat alien to artistic purity and aesthetic emotion."

————. *Estudios de historia literaria de España* (Madrid: Imprenta de la Revista Española, 1901), pp. 363-403. A long necrology read before the Spanish Royal Academy. Contains biographical information and a careful examination of most of the plays. Originally published in the *Revista de Archivos, Bibliotecas y Museos,* July 1898, pp. 289-319.

CROCKER, LESTER G. "Techniques in *Un drama nuevo,*" *Hispania* XXXIX (1956), 412-18. Argues that Tamayo's unmatched skill

in dramatic technique consists of the persistent play of ambiguities. A thorough examination of *Un drama nuevo.*

CUETO, LEOPOLDO AUGUSTO DE. *Estudios de historia y de crítica literaria* (Madrid: Rivadeneyra, 1900), pp. 391-436. Discusses
the Roman legend of Virginia in dramatic literature. Argues
that of the score or more Virginia plays in European literature,
Tamayo's is the best. Says that Tamayo's *Virginia* has only one
important defect, namely, Virginia's marriage to Icilio.

ECHEGARAY, JOSÉ. *Recuerdos,* I (Madrid: Ruiz Hermanos, 1917).
The memoirs of a famous playwright. Echegaray (1832-1916)
describes what happened when he saw Tamayo's *Ángela* (pp.
29-32) and *Lances de honor* (pp. 292-303). Many references
to the ideas, theater, and politics of the period. No index.

EOFF, SHERMAN H. "The Spanish Novel of Ideas, Critical Opinion
1836-1880)," *PMLA,* LV (1940), 532-58. Examines the thesis
novels (*novelas tendenciosas*) of the nineteenth century. Argues
that there was a mixture of moderate liberalism and conservatism,
then a "severe conservatism" following the mid-century, and
then a rather broad liberalism in the 1870's. Although this article
only studies the novel, it throws light on Tamayo's thesis plays,
which belong to Eoff's period of "severe conservatism."

ESQUER TORRES, RAMÓN. "Contribución al epistolario de Tamayo y
Baus," *Boletín de la Sociedad Castellonense de Cultura,* Cuaderno IV (1962), 377-97. Discusses and reproduces thirteen
letters written by Tamayo to various people. All but one pertain to the last twenty-five years of Tamayo's life, his "silent
period." Many footnotes.

—————. *El teatro de Tamayo y Baus* (Madrid: Consejo Superior de
Investigaciones Científicas, 1965). A thorough study of Tamayo's
theater by the leading *tamayista.*

—————. "Epistolario de Manuel Tamayo y Baus a Manuel Cañete,"
Revista de Literatura, II (julio-diciembre 1961), 367-405. The
most complete of the various letter collections. Fifty letters
from Tamayo, "Manuel #1," to his best friend and fellow academician, Manuel Cañete, "Manuel #2." (In keeping with his
last will, Tamayo's nephew destroyed nearly all of his letters
and papers.)

—————. "Las luchas del siglo XIX. El P. Blanco García y Leopoldo
Alas 'Clarín,'" *Boletín de la Sociedad Castellonense de Cultura,*
XXXVIII (1962), 241-55. Throws light on the ideological and
religious polemics of the late nineteenth century. Tamayo and
others backed the undistinguished Commelerán for a Royal
Academy chair rather than the great novelist, Galdós. Menén-

dez Pelayo backed Galdós, although he was, like Tamayo, a champion of Catholicism. "A most interesting era, but stormy and complex like few others."

——————. "Para un epistolario Tamayo y Baus—Asenjo Barbieri," *Boletín de la Real Academia Española,* Cuaderno CLXV, Tomo XLII (1962), 121-43. Discusses the friendship of Tamayo and the famous composer Francisco Asenjo-Barbieri (1823-1894). Reproduces thirty-one letters from Tamayo to his friend, on whom Tamayo relied for the definitions of musical terms in the Royal Academy dictionary.

——————. "Para un epistolario Tamayo—Menéndez Pelayo," *Boletín de la Biblioteca de Menéndez y Pelayo,* XXVIII (1962), 153-72. Twenty-four letters from Tamayo, the secretary of the Royal Academy, to Marcelino Menéndez Pelayo (1856-1912), its youngest and most erudite member. These letters show the devotion to duty and also the humor of Tamayo, who is apt to address his colleague as "young pup of my heart."

——————. "Para un epistolario Valera—Tamayo y Baus," *Boletín de la Real Academia Española,* XXXIX (1959), 89-163. Thirty-eight letters from Don Juan Valera (1824-1905) to Tamayo between 1882 and 1896. Written while Valera was an ambassador abroad. Throws light on Tamayo's silent period, during which he was secretary of the Royal Academy.

——————. "Tamayo y Baus: sus proyectos literarios inacabados," *Boletín de la Real Academia Española,* XLIII (1963), 151-64. Discusses fragments, titles, and notes found amongst Tamayo's papers. Says they were from plays and other works he thought of writing at one time or another. Attempts to list them chronologically.

——————. "Tamayo y Baus y la política del siglo XIX," *Segismundo: Revista Hispánica de Teatro,* I (1965), 71-91. Divides the political life of Tamayo into four stages. In three of these, he either had government assignments or a pension, but in only one of them was he an active participant in political affairs. After the Revolution of 1868, he became a Carlist for a brief period and ran unsuccessfully for office.

——————. "Tamayo y Baus y la Real Academia," *Boletín de la Real Academia,* XLIII (mayo-agosto 1962), 299-335. Contains a commentary and many letters about Tamayo's petition for entrance into the Academy, his acceptance speech, his pseudonyms, his hard work as secretary of the Academy, his death and eulogies.

——————. "Tamayo y Baus y Pedro Antonio de Alarcón," *Boletín de*

la Real Academia Española, XLIV (1963), 463-71. Discusses
the friendship of Tamayo, Alarcón, and other conservative members of the Royal Academy. Reproduces a prologue by Tamayo,
never before published, to a posthumous collection of Alarcón's
works.

————.Un aspecto desconocido de Tamayo y Baus: su obra lírica.
Castellón de la Plana, 1968. A collection of almost seventy pages
of Tamayo's verses never edited before. Includes sonnets, ter-
cets, redondillas, a fable, ditties written for albums and ladies'
fans, and the long poem "Spain Without Honor, an Epic Song
to the September Revolution." The prologue argues that Tamayo
is a born dramatist, and an able though not distinguished writer
of verses.

————. "Un cuento inédito de Tamayo y Baus," Boletín de la Biblioteca de Menéndez y Pelayo, XXXIX (1963), 195-207. The
author has discovered and published here a short story by
Tamayo which the latter calls a "semitrue novel." Throws light
on Tamayo's meticulous mode of writing.

————. "Una interesante carta de Tamayo y Baus," in Homenajes.
Estudios de Filología Española (1964), pp. 25-31. A long letter,
dated 1862, from Tamayo to Antonio Cánovas del Castillo
concerning an abuse within the theater. A national theater house
had been awarded to an inferior company.

FERNÁNDEZ FLÓREZ, ISIDORO. "Estudio crítico-biográfico de don Manuel Tamayo y Baus," in Pedro de Novo y Colson, Autores dramáticos contemporáneos y joyas del arte español del siglo XIX, II
(Madrid, 1886), 461-86. Discusses the major plays of Tamayo,
one by one. Argues that he willfully breaks his own aesthetic
credo; "even his errors are meditated." Says that his theater
shows an admiration of women and that he directs his theater
towards the good.

FERNÁNDEZ-GUERRA Y ORBE, AURELIANO. "Discurso de contestación,"
in Discursos leídos en las recepciones públicas que ha celebrado
desde 1847 la Real Academia Española. Tomo Segundo. (Madrid: Imprenta Nacional, 1860), 293-303. In this theocentric
speech, Tamayo's childhood friend welcomes him into the Royal
Academy. He argues that art must follow nature, using her
"inexhaustible treasures."

FITZ-GERALD, JOHN D. "Un drama nuevo on the American Stage,"
Hispania, VII (1924), 171-76. Concludes that there were two
American translations of this play in the 1870's, one by William Dean Howells. The author has been unable to find a copy
of these translations, both of which altered the plot; but a

translation that tried to take no liberties with the text was published by The Hispanic Society of America under the title *A New Drama*.

GOODELL, BLANCHE EMMA. "Manuel Tamayo y Baus, Sources and Aesthetics." University of Wisconsin, unpublished doctoral dissertation, 1950. Examines the plays Tamayo reworked from foreign sources, in an effort to determine his dramatic creed. Studies the changes he made: what he added or deleted. Argues that his plays do not always conform to the aesthetic credo set forth in his Royal Academy entrance speech.

GUENON, PIERRE. "En torno a dos cartas de X. Durrien y de J. G. Hugelmann," *Boletín de la Biblioteca de Menéndez y Pelayo*, XLI, (1965), 87-90. The author has found two French letters amongst the papers of Manuel Cañete, one of which refers to Victor Hugo, the other to Tamayo.

HOUSE, ROY TEMPLE. "Lope de Vega and *Un drama nuevo*," *Romanic Review*, XIII (1922), 84-87. A brief study in comparative literature. The author examines plays of Shakespeare, Kyd, Jean Rotrou, and Lope de Vega as possible sources of *Un drama nuevo*.

HUBBARD, GUSTAVE. *Histoire de la littérature contemporaine en Espagne* (Paris: Charpentier, 1876), pp. 228-34. Discusses two plays of Tamayo, *Virginia* and *La ricahembra*. Argues that *Virginia* suffers grave defects owing to Tamayo's antidemocratic bias. Prefers *La ricahembra*, a good play.

KRONIK, JOHN. "The Nineteenth-Century Spanish Drama and the Critic's Dilemma." An unpublished address delivered at the 1971 convention of the Modern Language Association in Chicago, Illinois. Argues that Hispanists have failed in their responsibility to the nineteenth-century Spanish theater in all areas beyond the purely historical and descriptive. Criticism has been positivistic and has ignored the fact that literature is a continuum. Lack of sympathy for a rhetorical mode or ethical mode, such as Tamayo's, does not excuse the slighting of an entire genre. (Copies of this address are available from the author, who teaches at Cornell University, Ithaca, New York.)

LÓPEZ DE AYALA, ADELARDO. *Obras*, I (Madrid: Imprenta de Pérez Dubrull, 1881). Tamayo and Manuel Cañete edited the works of the deceased playwright, López de Ayala. In his introduction, Tamayo reiterates his own aesthetic creed when he speaks of López de Ayala's plays, "works in which the beautiful and the good go hand in hand, mastering souls, both delighting them and exalting them."

LOTT, ROBERT E. "On Mannerism and Mannered Approaches to Realism in *Un drama nuevo, Consuelo,* and Earlier Nineteenth-Century Plays," *Hispania,* LIV (1971), 844-55. Discusses theories of style and the problem of mannerism vis-à-vis realism in the drama of the nineteenth century, with special emphasis on the *alta comedia.* Argues that the dramatists did not develop "a genuine period style," one that successfully intuits the quality of human experience peculiar to the day, one that phrases it in forms "deeply congenial to the thought, science, and technology which are part of that experience. . . . Says that *Un drama nuevo* is "an irritatingly mannered play."

MAZZEO, GUIDO E. "Yorick's Covert Motives in *Un drama nuevo,*" *Modern Language Notes,* LXXXIII (1968), 275-78. Argues that Yorick had a covert, undeclared desire to portray a betrayed husband; that before receiving the part of Count Octavio he was suspicious of his wife's love for Edmundo.

MÉNDEZ BEJARANO, MARIO. *La literatura española en el siglo XIX* (Madrid: Gráfica Universal, 1921), Chapter VI. Argues that Tamayo, "a superior mind," was excessively influenced by foreign muses—French, Italian, English, and German. Therefore, although a great playwright, he must cede the dramatic crown of the nineteenth century to Adelardo López de Ayala.

NERVO, AMADO. "Un drama nuevo," in *Obras completas,* I, 4a. edición (Madrid: Editorial Aguilar, 1967), 480-81. A brief review of this play, which was staged in Mexico in February, 1895.

NOCEDAL, CÁNDIDO. *Discurso.* In *Discursos leídos en las recepciones públicas que ha celebrado desde 1847 la Real Academia Española.* Tomo Segundo (Madrid: Imprenta Nacional, 1860), 371-414. The speech that Nocedal, Tamayo's close friend, read on entering the Academy, and also the Duke of Rivas' reply. Discusses the use and abuse of the novel, the idea of "to delight instructing, and instruct delighting," and the need of discretion. Throws light on Tamayo's stance in his thesis plays, which are like thesis novels.

PAR, ALFONSO. *Shakespeare en la literatura española.* Biblioteca Balmes (Barcelona: Victoriano Suárez 1935). Says that Tamayo is the Spanish author who moved most constantly within "the air of the poet of Stratford." Negatively criticizes Tamayo's acceptance speech on entering the Royal Academy.

PODOL, PETER L. "The Evolution of the Honor Theme in Modern Spanish Drama," *Hispanic Review,* XL (1972), 53-72. Argues that the *alta comedia* "contains all of the antecedents for the total repudiation of traditional honor." Discusses Tamayo's *Lances de honor* and *Un drama nuevo.*

QUALIA, CHARLES B. "The *Raisonneur* in the Social Drama of Spain from Tamayo to Linares Rivas," *Hispania,* XIX (1936), 407-14. The *raisonneur* in the social drama is the character who moralizes. Argues that Tamayo's *raisonneurs* are old-fashioned moralizers who voice in unmistaken terms the author's social theories: honor, adherence to the letter of Catholic ethics, righteousness in the face of the strongest temptation or opposition.

REVILLA, MANUEL DE LA. "Bocetos literarios. Don Manuel Tamayo y Baus," in the *Revista contemporánea,* X (1877), 500-505. A contemporary assessment of Tamayo's significance. Argues that Tamayo rejects the excesses of both neo-Classicism and Romanticism. He represents "the discretion, the delicate taste and the reasonable realism of the classical theater, and the liberty, the high flight, and the rich inspiration of the Romantic theater." Deplores Tamayo's ultraconservative politics. Has a very high regard for him as a person: pure, noble, and gentle.

RODRÍGUEZ RUBÍ, TOMÁS. *Discurso.* In *Discursos leídos en las recepciones públicas que ha celebrado desde 1847 la Real Academia Española,* II (Madrid: Imprenta Nacional, 1860), 417-43. Argues that the theater is both a *school* and a *reflection* of customs. As a school it teaches, as a reflection it delights. Argues that the contemporary (1860) European theater is suffering from materialism, a suppression of the spirit. The Spanish theater, which is sick, though not dead, needs the protection of the law against industrialism. A companion of Tamayo in the Academy, Rodríguez Rubí presents ideas similar to those of Tamayo's moral dramas.

ROGERS, PAUL PATRICK. "Galdós and Tamayo's Letter-Substitution Device," *Romanic Review,* XLV, (1954), 115-20. Argues that in *Un drama nuevo* Tamayo is perhaps the only playwright in history who used the "substitution device" of a real letter for a blank stage prop. Says that Galdós imitated Tamayo in his novel, *La corte de Carlos IV.*

————. *The Spanish Drama Collection in the Oberlin College Library. A Descriptive Catalogue* (Oberlin, 1940). Describes 7530 Spanish plays in the Oberlin College Library. Lists several Tamayo plays not in the *Obras completas,* viz., *El castillo de Balsaín, El cinco de agosto, El don del cielo, Don Simplicio Bobadilla, Una aventura de Richelieu, Tran-Tran.* Also lists plays by Tamayo's brothers, Andrés and Victorino.

ROS, FELIX. *Notas sobre literatura* (Madrid: Ediciones Cultura Hispánica, 1950), pp. 273-77. Brief article declaring that Tamayo is unjustly forgotten today. Emphasizes Tamayo's aesthetic credo: "Man, and above man, God."

RUIZ RAMÓN, FRANCISCO. *Historia del teatro español (desde sus orígenes hasta 1900)* (Madrid: Alianza Editorial, 1967), pp. 444-54. Explains the meaning of the *alta comedia* of Ventura de la Vega, Tamayo, and López de Ayala. Argues that their *alta comedia* has "a will for dramatic realism," but nevertheless leaves "the impression of falseness and unreality." Argues that the schemes are too simplistic. Has, moreover, a low opinion of Tamayo's *Virginia*, a high opinion of *Un drama nuevo*.

SAINZ DE ROBLES, FEDERICO CARLOS. *Ensayo de un diccionario de literatura.* 3a. edición (Madrid: Editorial Aguilar, 1964), II, 1132-34. A concise account of Tamayo's life and writings. Cites several nineteenth-century critics.

SCHWARZ, EGON. "Manuel Tamayo y Baus and Schiller," *Comparative Literature*, XIII (1961), 123-37. Carefully examines the influence of Schiller's *Jungfrau von Orleans* and *Kabale und Liebe* on Tamayo's *Juana de Arco* and *Ángela*. Tamayo's *Juana de Arco* has less of the miraculous than Schiller's play, and his *Ángela* is less rhetorical and grandiloquent than *Kabale und Liebe*.

SHAW, D. L. "*Humorismo* and *Angustia* in Modern Spanish Literature," *Bulletin of Hispanic Studies*, XXXV (1958), 165-76. Argues that the *humorismo* of the Romantics and the Generation of 1898, a sort of metaphysical gallows humor, is based on a spiritual contradiction. Life is tragic and one must have an escape. Tamayo experienced no such spiritual contradiction and so had no metaphysical dilemma to escape from. Gives a clear insight into nineteenth-century literature as a whole.

————. "The Anti-Romantic Reaction in Spain." *Modern Language Review*, LXIII (1968), 606-11. Argues that the Romantic writers, in spite of their splendor, were in a minority. Romanticism was in essence revolutionary, and a call was made for a literature based on wholesome doctrines. One of those who both made and answered this call was Manuel Tamayo y Baus.

————. "Towards the Understanding of Spanish Romanticism," *Modern Language Review*, LVIII (1963), 190-95. Shows how for many nineteenth-century Spaniards there was no choice between orthodoxy and the void. Helps the reader to understand Tamayo, a "neo-Catholic" who championed orthodoxy against the void in his thesis dramas.

SICARS Y SALVADÓ, NARCISO. *D. Manuel Tamayo y Baus. Estudio crítico-biográfico* (Barcelona: Tipografía Católica, 1906). A long (426 pages) encomiastic study of Tamayo, "the immortal author of *Virginia, La locura de amor, Lances de honor,* and *Un drama nuevo.*" Calls the nineteenth century "the great century of dramatic poetry." Says that Tamayo's *Lo positivo* and López de Ayala's *El tanto por ciento* created "the drama of contemporary customs or *alta comedia* in which there are so happily combined the most moderate and acceptable of Romantic audacities with the polish and correction of Classicism, what is profoundly Spanish in character with the exigencies of the modern era." This statement will serve as a definition of the *alta comedia.*

SMITH, W. F. "Contributions of Rodríguez Rubí to the Development of the *Alta Comedia," Hispanic Review,* X (1942), 53-63. Describes the *alta comedia* of Tamayo and López de Ayala, which is concerned with the elegant and refined upper middle class. The language of these comedies is sober, elegant, and pure. What most distinguished them is their didactic note. Sees Tomás Rodríguez Rubí (1817-1890) as the precursor of Tamayo and López de Ayala.

TANNENBERG, BORIS DE. *L'Espagne Littéraire* (Paris: Picard et Fils, 1903), pp. 1-84. Argues that about 1850 a reaction began against the extravagance of Romanticism. It is the period of the school of good sense, characterized by a greater concern for proportion, taste, and truth in art; sometimes this leads to prosaism. It is the period of Adelardo López de Ayala, and Tamayo. Says that Tamayo is the enemy of a pretentious style, that he has "a lapidary precision." Studies his major plays, one by one.

TAYLER, NEALE H. "Manuel Tamayo y Baus: Some Early Influences," *Hispania,* XXV (1952), 395-98. Discusses the influence of Schiller and Hugo on Tamayo.

––––––. *Las fuentes del teatro de Tamayo y Baus. Originalidad e influencias.* (Madrid: Gráficas Uguina, 1959). Studies the sources of Tamayo's works and also other literary influences. One chapter discusses Tamayo's theatrical theory, the others, Tamayo and the German, Spanish, French, and English theaters.

VALBUENA PRAT, ÁNGEL. *Historia del teatro español* (Barcelona: Editorial Noguer, 1956), pp. 527-39. Argues that Tamayo and Adelardo López de Ayala are the two central figures of the realistic theater in Spain. Argues that Tamayo's plays only meet his realistic credo halfway. Very high praise for *Un drama nuevo,* scant praise for his other works: "one too readily detects the hand of the director moving the dolls of his puppet show."

—————. *El sentido católico en la literatura española* (Zaragoza: Ediciones Partenón, 1960), pp. 147-67. These pages discuss the literature of the nineteenth century and Catholicism. They say that Tamayo was a Catholic of the movement in literature known as Realism. His dramatic slogan was "man, and above man, God." However, there is a "crisis of realization" and Tamayo's work does not measure up to his intentions. His thesis plays reveal the intransigent other-worldist rather than the serene theologian that Calderón was, or Tirso.

VALERA, JUAN. "La bola de nieve," in *Obras completas,* II (Madrid: Editorial Aguilar, 1942), 56-61. An article reviewing *La bola de nieve* and defending it against those critics who attacked it. Argues that *La bola de nieve* is one of the best dramas of the modern Spanish theater.

Index

155